T0209711

How to Raise an Abel When the World Is Raising Cain

Parenting by the Book

Keith D. Pisani

WESTBOW
P R E S S®
A DIVISION OF THOMAS NELSON
& ZONDERVAN

WestBow Press books may be ordered through booksellers or by contacting:

WestBow Press
A Division of Thomas Nelson & Zondervan
1663 Liberty Drive
Bloomington, IN 47403
www.westbowpress.com
1 (866) 928-1240

Interior Image Credit: Keith D. Pisani

Scripture taken from the King James Version of the Bible.

ISBN: 978-1-9736-8111-3 (sc)
ISBN: 978-1-9736-8110-6 (e)

Library of Congress Control Number: 2019919468

Print information available on the last page.

WestBow Press rev. date: 12/5/2019

Preface

IN DEMONSTRATING GOD'S LOVE FOR children, Jesus said, "Suffer [the] little children, and forbid them not (do not hinder them), to come unto Me: for of such is the kingdom of heaven" (Matthew 19:14).[1] Since Jesus places a high value on children, so should we.

In giving His counsel to parents, God's Holy Spirit gave this advice, "[Do not "hide/conceal" God's Law] from [your] children … telling to the "generation to come" the praises of the LORD, and His strength and His wonderful works that He has done" (Psalm 78:1–4). In addition, a father added, "This will be written for the "generation to come," that a people yet to be created may praise the Lord" (Psalm 102:18). What is the ultimate role of a parent? It is to disciple ("tell by teaching") his/her children … who will disciple ("tell by teaching") his/her children … who will disciple ("tell by teaching") the "generation to come" (which is "a generation yet unborn"). Because of their influence and effect on the children born to their children—for one set of parents to reach three additional generations—the original "first generation" set of parents must prioritize the discipling of their "generation of children"—for Christ—as their #1 responsibility in the home.

As the Father of all believers, God is the best parent of all. Although many have said that children do not come with instructions, they do. In His child-raising instruction book (the Bible), God gave parents His guidance on how to raise and disciple children successfully for God.[2]

With four children of our own, we thank God that each is living for the Lord. We pray that your children will be more like Abel and less like Cain as they grow into maturity for the Lord.[3]

Keith and Beth Pisani

Special note: In addition to the main text in this parenting manual, please take the time to read the additional material in the endnotes. The endnotes material adds a deeper layer of insights into the text. Thank you!

A List of Themes from the Passages that Appear in:
How to Raise an Abel when the World Is Raising Cain
(Passages are listed sequentially, as they appear in the text)

Text	Topic
Genesis 4:1	A parent's expectations
Genesis 4:2, Genesis 5:3–5	Having children (the number)
Genesis 4:3–5a	Children who honor/dishonor God
2 Timothy 4:3–4	Children who turn away from God
2 Timothy 4:3–4	Children who turn aside from God
Jude 4–13	Children who defect from the faith
Jude 17–23	How children can keep themselves faithful

Text	Topic
Ecclesiastes 1:2	A parent's lament: society's values
Proverbs 1:1–4	Ten reasons why God gave children parents
Proverbs 1:7–9	Respect for authority
Proverbs 1:10–16	Monitoring the influence of peer groups
Proverbs 2:1–5	Factors that determine a child's life direction
Proverbs 3:1–6	Trusting the guide book (the Bible)
Proverbs 3:11–12	A child's response to healthy discipline
Proverbs 3:21–26	Effects of bad decisions on the child/parent
Proverbs 4:1–9	Parent/child responsibilities
Proverbs 4:10–13, 20–23	The blessings of obedience
Proverbs 5:1–8. 20	The crowd your child keeps/immorality
Proverbs 6:1–5, 20–23	Wise money management
Proverbs 7:1–3, 24–27	Repeating/not repeating a parent's mistakes
Proverbs 8:1–4, 32	Keeping your spiritual commitments current
Proverbs 10:1, 5	A child's work ethic: laziness
Proverbs 13:1, 14	Humoring/honoring your parents

Text	Topic
Genesis 1:28–29; 9:1	wants families to have children
Genesis 12:3; Galatians 3:13–29	It is a blessing to lead your children to Christ
Genesis 18:19	Guarding your children for God
Genesis 22:1–14; Hebrews 11:17–19	The sacrifices of parents

Genesis 37:1–2, 1 Samuel 16:1–15, Acts 10:34, Romans 2:11, Proverbs 28:21	Play no favorites
Exodus 2:1–10; Hebrews 11:10, 23–29	God's "worst" is better than society's best
Exodus 20:1–5, 34:6–7; Numbers 14:18; Malachi 4:4–6	Godly parents are a blessing
Deuteronomy 6:4–9, 11:19; Psalm 128:1–4; Judges 2:10; 1 Thessalonians 2:7–9	"Priority parenting"
Deuteronomy 32:11–12a; Genesis 2:24, 12:1–2; Matthew 19:5; John 3:16–17; Ephesians 5:31	Children leaving the nest
Joshua 24:15; Isaiah 54:13; 3 John 4	Teaching your children to serve
1 Samuel 1–12; Judges 13:2–5, 24–25; 2 Peter 1:8; Psalm 113:9; Jeremiah 1:5	Motherhood
1 Samuel 2:12, 17; 2 Samuel 12:24, 14:28, 15:10; 2 Samuel 13; 1 Kings 1–2; Proverbs 1:8–9, 13:24, 23:13–14, 29:15, 17; Luke 15:11–32; Hebrews 12:6	Discipline/parental neglect: ungodly children
Psalm 127:1–5, 139:13–16, 128:1–4	Why God gave children parents
Proverbs 1:1–7, 3:1–6, 22:1–6; 1 Peter 2:2–3	Godly impressions: children are "wet cement"
Micah 6:7; Judges 11:30–40; Psalm 139:13–16; Jeremiah 1:5	All lives are sacred: born and unborn
Matthew 10:13–16, 18:2–6, 10, 19:14; Mark 9:36–37; Luke 17:1–2; 2 Timothy 1:5	Leading your children to Christ
Ephesians 6:1–4; Colossians 3:20; Proverbs 1:8 91; Timothy 4:12–13; Luke 2:40–52	Blessed obedience
1 Timothy 4:12–13; Titus 2:3–5, 5–8; Luke 2:40–52	A godly example: make it a pattern in life

History's First Children: Cain and Abel

The births of history's first children are recorded in Genesis 4. In living out obedience to God's command to "be fruitful, and multiply, and replenish the earth" (Genesis 1:28),

> Adam knew Eve his wife, and she conceived and bore Cain, and said, "I have [acquired] a man from the LORD." Then she bore again, this time his brother Abel. Now Abel was a keeper of sheep, but Cain was a tiller of the ground. And in the process of time it came to pass that Cain brought an offering of the fruit of the ground to the LORD. Abel also brought of the firstborn of his flock and of their fat. And the LORD respected Abel and his offering, but [He did not respect] Cain and his offering. And Cain was very [angry], and his countenance fell … And it came to pass, when they were in the field, that Cain rose up against Abel his brother and killed him … [Cain was] cursed from the earth. (Genesis 4:1–5, 8, 11)

I have sometimes wondered what it was like for history's first couple, Adam and Eve, to wake up the morning after the Fall and realize they had been banished from Paradise—with angels guarding the door (Genesis 3:24)—so they could see in but not get in. And then they had to spend 930 more years of life regretting their decision to disobey God, taste the forbidden fruit, and sin against the Lord. One bad decision led to a lifetime of grief. Yet with the constant reminder of epic failure always before them, Adam and Eve must have looked at each other, studied God's commandments, and said, "Even though we sinned and messed up royally in the past, let's obey God in something. Let's be fruitful and multiply. Let's have kids!"⁴ So they did.

Two sons! Conceived *after* humanity's Fall into sin,⁵ one son was a farmer focused on the land. The other was a shepherd sustaining the lives entrusted to his care. As humanity's first provider, Cain dug ditches, planted seeds, brought water to irrigate the ground, and through individual effort and the sweat of his brow, fed his world. As history's first pastor, Abel spent his days learning leadership: feeding, leading, and tending a flock of sheep. The first son made daily sacrifices that resulted in a harvest. The second son raised the sacrifices that his family would offer to God. Perhaps expecting Cain to be the promised Deliverer of Genesis 3:15, when Adam and Eve named their first child, they were so excited that Eve proclaimed, "I have gotten a man—even the Lord," and named him, "Acquired of God."[6] But even though he was hardworking and conscientious, Cain was no Deliverer. Perhaps disillusioned and with dashed expectations, history's first parents called their second son Abel. His name means "vanity/emptiness/futility" (Genesis 4:2).

Vanity! Emptiness! Futility! Think about the meaning of that name. When Eve called her second son Abel, did she name him out of the frustrations she experienced in raising her first son, Cain? Was it fair for Abel to go through life with a name that represented the negatives of the dashed expectations that Eve may have experienced in raising Cain? Since modern-day parents sometimes have a second child because the first child did not work out as planned, wasn't what they expected, or didn't live up to hopes, is it possible that Adam and Eve's frustration with their first child increased their motivation to "be fruitful and multiply" again? If that is the case, how often, in our current society, do the joys of having a newborn give way to the frustrations of raising that baby into adulthood, knowing that every child—as a descendant of Adam and Eve—is born with a nature to sin (Romans 5:12, 19; 1 Corinthians 15:33; Psalm 51:5)? Because every child and parent shares in that original sin nature, is it possible for parents to successfully raise children, especially for the Lord?

Knowing that it is possible to raise children for the Lord, what lessons can modern-day parents learn from scripture's Genesis account of Cain and Abel?

First, it is common for parents to expect great things from their children (Genesis 4:1).

Of history's first birth announcement, "I have acquired a man from the Lord," it may be possible to translate the last portion of Eve's expression of joy in childbirth as "I have acquired a man—*even the Lord.*" If this is the case, then Eve took God's promise to provide a Deliverer literally (Genesis 3:15). Knowing that God's promised Deliverer had to be more powerful—with greater authority—than the serpent Satan, is it possible that Eve believed that she, not Mary, had given birth to humanity's promised Savior? Yet just as every modern-day baby does not become a president, a doctor, or a lawyer, Cain was no Christ. Cain was a sinner. Only Jesus saves.

As a parent, be realistic in your expectations. Allow God to work out His plan and accomplish His will for your child's life. Refuse to become bitter or resentful if your child does not live up to your hopes or your dreams for his or her life. Help your child discover God's purpose for his or her life and to form a salvation relationship with God through faith in Jesus, to give God glory, and to be faithful to Him.

Second, God establishes the number of children each couple should have (Genesis 4:2, 5:3–5).

Adam and Eve had more children after Cain and Abel (Genesis 4:2). They had a third son, Seth (Genesis 5:4), and other sons (plural) and daughters (plural).

Then she bore again, this time his brother Abel. (Genesis 4:2)

And Adam lived one hundred and thirty years, and begot *a son* in his own likeness, after his image, and named him Seth. After he begot Seth, the days of Adam were eight hundred years; and he had sons and daughters. (Genesis 5:3–4)

Not every couple will have children. Not every set of parents will have more than one child. Yet the multiplication of the human race is a vital part of God's plan (Genesis 3:15)—whether biologically or through adoption. Assuming that Cain and Abel were not twins, and recognizing the possibility that, as Cain became older, he was not the perfect child, did the thought of limiting the first family to one child instead of many enter the first parents' minds?

In response, Adam and Eve already had disobeyed God's command to "not eat" of the tree of the knowledge of good and evil (Genesis 2:16–17). For that, they suffered consequences. Did history's first couple also want to risk the consequences of disobeying God's command to be "fruitful and multiply and replenish the earth"? The obvious answer is no.

If the story of Adam and Eve played out in modern times, would modern-day Eve consider an abortion of her second child? Knowing that a holy God could have killed both Adam and Eve immediately after their Fall[7] but instead, in love, did not consider Adam and Eve a mistake but spared their lives by grace, Eve said no to Abel's abortion and yes to Abel's life.[8] Perhaps God had Eve in mind when His prophet wrote, "Shall I give my firstborn *for* my transgression, the fruit of my body *for* the sin of my soul?" (Micah 6:7). Eve said no! So should we.

1. God wants His children to honor Him (Genesis 4:3–5a).

And in the process of time it came to pass that Cain brought an offering of the fruit of the ground to the LORD. Abel also brought of the firstborn of his flock and of their fat. And the LORD respected Abel and his offering, but He did not respect Cain and his offering." (Genesis 4:3–5a)

By bringing the work of God's hands—an animal—Abel's sacrifice was accepted because "without the shedding of blood, there is no remission (forgiveness) of sins" (Hebrews 9:22). In bringing his offering from ground that was cursed (see Genesis 2:17–18), Cain's offering was refused because he brought the work of his own hands, which represented the pride of man-centered, works-oriented, performance-based religion—a religion that God condemns (see Titus 3:5–6). Recognizing that faith in the shed blood of a sacrifice is the only approach to God that God accepts,[9] Abel approached God on God's terms. Cain approached God on Cain's terms. God rejected the offering of Cain. Angry at God's rejection, Cain committed history's first sin involving a man against a man. The brother who neglected to kill an animal as his sacrifice had no difficulty shedding the blood of his brother. Cain murdered Abel (see 1 John 3:12, 15). In killing Abel who was right (righteous) with God, though he is dead, Abel's obedience to God yet speaks (Hebrews 11:4). In what way(s) does Abel's "double-blood" sacrifice (of his animal and of himself) yet speak? Because we sinners cannot please God on our own terms, God does not want an offering from the works of our hands. He demands a sacrifice. Pride-filled, man-centered, works-oriented, performance-based religion is man's attempt to bypass the righteous demands of a Holy God. God's requirement for man's redemption is through faith in Christ's blood that He shed at Calvary (Romans 3:24–25). Because of Christ's sacrifice, we have "redemption through His blood, the forgiveness of sins, according to the riches of His grace" (Ephesians 1:7). Unlike Cain who—through offering the fruit of a cursed earth, the product of his labors, and the sweat of his brow—ignored the future sacrifice of Christ at Calvary, sinners should never ignore the same sacrifice that Christ made two thousand plus years ago on His cross. Sinners need a blood sacrifice. The only blood sacrifice that pleases God today is the Lamb for sinners slain: Jesus. In acknowledging Abel's recognition of the value of a blood sacrifice approved by God, Abel was privileged to become the first person in history to go to heaven ("Upper Sheol"/"Paradise" in Old Testament times). In making sure that the story of his faithfulness would be known and repeated to the generations to come, God chose Abel to be the first to be inducted into scripture's Hall of Fame.[10] Since death is never the last word in the life of a godly man, "being dead, Abel yet speaks" (Hebrews 11:4).

If any book in the Bible describes the "way of Cain," it is that New Testament postcard Jude, which states,

> Woe to them! For they have gone in the way of Cain, have run greedily in the error of Balaam for profit, and perished in the rebellion of Korah. But (in contrast to Cain, Balaam, and Korah) you, beloved, building yourselves up on your most holy faith, praying in the Holy Spirit, keep yourselves in the love of God, looking for the mercy of our Lord Jesus Christ unto eternal life. (Jude 11:20–21)

The "way of Cain" is that approach to life that turns its ears away from the truth and turns aside to [its own way] (2 Timothy 4:3–4). With this in mind, two phrases must be examined.

2 Timothy 4:3–4. The phrase: "turn away"

The phrase "turn away" (the Greek term *apostrepho*) is the root for the English word *apostrophe*, which is a shortened (abbreviated) form of a fuller word or a greater reality. As a term, the word *apostrophe* was used in Matthew 26:52 of returning a sword to its sheath. Having taken out the Sword of the Spirit, which is the Word of the Lord, and even having used it in spiritual battle, there are people who once professed faith in Christ who return the Word to its sheath and move on ("away from") the gospel that saved them. Every generation experiences children who, once they leave their parents' home, walk away from the truth. The term *apostrophe* appears in Matthew 27:3, where it is used of the "other" Judas—Judas Iscariot—who, once he realized that his act of betrayal condemned him for eternity, mentally/emotionally regretted ("turned away from") his betrayal and returned the price of his apostasy ($14 American/thirty pieces of silver) to the priests of his former religion. But, for Judas, his regret was not repentance. Having never returned to fully following Christ, as one who "turned away," Judas is spending his eternity in "his own place," which is a place that burns with fire (see Acts 1:25).[11] Just because a child is raised in a religious setting or has parents who walk with Christ, there is no guarantee that the child will not, as an adult, live out an "abbreviated" form of faith. Judas walked and talked with Jesus (see Mark 3:14). Yet Judas fell short in his faith. If falling short in faith can happen to one who was taught by Christ directly, then children of godly parents can fall short too. In Titus 1:14, the term *apostrophe* is used of people "turning away from" scripture as the believer's absolute authority for all things faith and for all things practice. Let there be no confusion: to be truth, it is not enough for a statement to resemble the truth. Because "God's Word is truth" (see John 17:17), opinions, philosophies, and perspectives must be consistent with God's Truth to be truth. When Cain decided to offer an "inconsistent-with-Truth" sacrifice (see Genesis 4:3–5a), God rejected it. Children must be aware that Christ, not the crowd, represents truth. Then, in Hebrews 12:25, the term *apostrophe* is used of "turning away from" Jesus and from those who speak His name. There is only one gospel. Since God owns heaven, no person has the right to change the gospel the God of heaven gave. Anyone who "turns away from" the gospel "turns away from" Jesus. In contrast, if there is a "spiritual apostrophe" that genuine believers *should* experience, it is the "apostrophe/turning away from" the ungodliness of Romans 11:26, which is away from the way of Cain to the way of Christ. Paul made that clear when he used the term *apostrophe* again when, in Romans 12:9, he wrote, "Abhor (turn away from) evil" and "cleave (become glued) to that which is good" (so that the child of God and the good become inseparable). When a child makes an act of the will and chooses to sin, he/she has walked already through the door that leads to the desk where the devil "signs that child up" for a full-fledged "turning away from" God's truth. Just as an apostrophe in language arts is used to shorten a word, people who make an "apostrophe" ("turn away from") of the truth, practice an abbreviated form of faith that falls short of total commitment, consistent faithfulness, or full surrender. Because there is no substitute for the one Substitute Who is Jesus, when children seek to replace the Calvary sacrifice of Jesus with their own forms of "spiritual sacrifice"—as with Cain—their "substitute sacrifice" will be rejected too.

2 Timothy 4:3–4. The phrase "turn aside"

From 2 Timothy 4:3–4, the phrase *turn aside* (The Greek term *extrero*—a word that references one "on the way to apostasy" and means "to stray or to walk with a limp due to a sprain") was used in 1

Timothy 1:6 of people who claim to know Christ as Savior, yet are "turned aside" by the "vain janglings" (ringing bells; attracting noises) of this world. When a bell is rung, the noise automatically draws a person's attention. You look. You investigate the cause of the ringing of the bell. Then, drawn to the cause or to the activity the bell announces, the person who responds invests his/her life in pursuits that do not receive God's blessing. When, under the inspiration of God, the prophet wrote, in 1 Samuel 2:30b, that "those who honor Me I will honor, and those who despise Me shall be lightly esteemed," the term *honor* speaks of "value." The Hebrew phrase "lightly esteemed" is: "*ye-qal-lu*," which means "brought low, not highly regarded," or "lacking respect" and was used forty times in the Old Testament of "being cursed." Even today, God places a high value on those who place a high value on Him and renders less respect to children who hold God and His authorities in contempt.[12] When a child devalues his/her relationship with God or the authority of God's Word, what response should that child expect from God—honor and blessing or dishonor and a lack of respect from God? The term *apostasy* is used also in 1 Timothy 6:20–21, where Paul addressed his son in the faith by stating, "O Timothy! Guard (place a sentinel on) what was committed to your trust, avoiding the profane *and* idle babblings and contradictions of what is falsely called knowledge—by professing it some have strayed concerning the faith" (1 Timothy 6:20–21). "Profane babblings" includes blasphemous speech that denies the authority of God. Although elevated by society to opinions worth considering, "vain babblings" is empty speech that has no biblical support. Regardless of their modern-day acceptance, both forms of "babbling utterances" mock the character of God and lend themselves to a science ("knowledge") falsely called—a science that, in God's eyes, is not science at all (1 Timothy 6:20). Just because a child gives "lip service" to his or her parents' faith does not mean that the child is truly saved. One reason that God gave children parents is that parents can lead their children to a genuine saving knowledge of Jesus Christ at the earliest possible age and then disciple those children so that they will grow into spiritual adulthood as practicing believers. Based on these God-given purposes, parents should quiz their children about their salvation experience and provide "new convert" follow-up by discipling their children for Christ.[13] Since most Western parents only have direct access with their children for eighteen years, every parent must be both an evangelist and a discipler. This way, children will walk with strength and not with a "spiritual limp" (in this context, to "walk with a spiritual limp" is the meaning of the Greek term *extrero*).

Since many parents experience the heartache of having a child "turn away from" or "turn aside from" the truth, what characterizes children who defect, depart, disappear, leave, or fall away from their faith?

Jude 4–13. Characteristics of children who "defect" or "depart from" the faith

1. They do not live a Christ-like life (Jude 4). They are ungodly.
2. They make a disgrace of grace (Jude 4). They use the grace of God as an excuse for unbridled lust, for a lack of respect for "things that are spiritual," and for living a life of no moral restraint.

3. By their actions, they mark themselves (predispose themselves) for judgment (Jude 4). Both children and parents must recognize that their ultimate accountability is to the only eternal authority in their life: the One True God.

4. They ignore the fact that, in their relationship with Christ, lip service is not life (Jude 5). A mere profession of faith is not the same as possessing genuine salvation.

5. They experience the privileges associated with salvation, but, in rebellion that leads to judgment, they choose another way (Jude 6). God's created angels had the honor of standing in the presence of God Himself, yet one third of those angels despised that privilege, followed Satan, and sought their own way. Children are born with crooked haloes. They will seek their way. Pull them back from the judgment. In love, be stronger than their strongest moments. Hold them accountable to God.

6. They are unrestrained in sin (Jude 7). They are like the people of Sodom and Gomorrah (Jude 7) who gave themselves over to "fornication" by substituting their ways for God's way as they lived for the flesh and not in the power of God's Holy Spirit.[14] Only Jesus gives His followers the strength to live in the resurrection power that keeps His children from falling so that each can avoid God's judgment and be presented as faultless before His presence in glory with exceeding joy (see Jude 24).

7. They know the truth but rarely apply it (Jude 11). They are self-willed like Cain, who substituted his own gospel for the gospel of God. In Genesis 4:3–5a, God's required sacrifice was a blood sacrifice. But, in pride, Cain brought the works of his hands and not the work of God's grace. This action of "replacing God's Substitute Jesus with man's substitutes/ religions" is the basis of all "substitute systems of faith" that exist in society. It is a look-at-me pride-centered approach to God that elevates the works of man while ignoring the grace of God. Beware of "the way of Cain."

8. They are nominally religious like Balaam, who knew enough of the truth to have a conversation about God but not enough of the truth to allow it to change his life (Jude 11). A child cannot both curse (mock) the faith and/or standards of God's people and truly honor (value) God.

9. They stand in the way of spiritual progress and truth (Jude 11). Just as Moses and Aaron were God's appointed leaders for Israel, dad and mom are God's appointed leaders in the home (Ephesians 6:1–4). Unlike Sanballat, Tobiah, and Geshem, who opposed the work of God as carried out by Nehemiah (Nehemiah 2); Shimei, who cursed (mocked) David (2 Samuel 16:5–13); Euodias and Syntiche, who saw themselves as an equal to or greater in authority than God (Philippians 4:1–2); Jannes and Jambres of Exodus 7 who, in their attempt to prevent the deliverance of God's people, grieved, resisted, and quenched the will and Spirit of God (2 Timothy 3:8); Alexander the Coppersmith who vigorously opposed the Word of God presented by Paul and the work of God practiced by Paul and he did it to Paul's

face (2 Timothy 4:14–15); Diotrephes, who thought he "ruled the roost" (3 John 9–11); and like Korah, who rebelled against authority and stood in the way of truth (Numbers 16:21), there are children who think they know best and who stand against the leadership of the parents whom God has appointed and established in the home. Children bear the character of the apostate (like those listed above) when they yield to the influence of people like Korah and others, in the Bible, who stood in the way of God's blessings when they tempted believers to reject God's truth. To be honored by God, children must practice obedience to God's truth—regardless of any contrary influences around them.

10. They are concerned for self, not others (Jude 12). Like the people at feasts who satisfy their own appetites while neglecting the needs of others (feeding themselves without regard for others), spoiled/entitled/self-absorbed children think of themselves first, last, and always. They grab the largest apple in the fruit basket and live on candy at the feasts. As Christ thought of others, so should we (see Philippians 2:5–8).[15]

11. They are all show but little substance (Jude 12). Windbags are deceptive. As empty clouds that hold no water, carried about by winds, they talk the talk but lack a walk for Jesus. Like clouds that hold no water, they promise much but deliver little. Living as spiritual hypocrites in the home, they are merely shells of the real spiritual thing. Parents need to get to know their children by what their children do and not by what their children say. Watch out for people who have a form of godliness yet deny the power behind that godliness—God Himself.

12. There is no evidence of salvation. Lacking spiritual fruit, they look good on the outside, but their hearts are far from God (Jude 12). They are dead and fruitless trees. Where there is no fruit for Christ, there is no root in Christ. God wants fruit not foliage.

13. They want to make a good impression and keep up appearances, yet they live a double life (Jude 13). They are foaming waves—like wild waves in the sea. If you have you ever been to an ocean's beach before, during, or just after a storm, you know that the waves are monstrous and what they leave behind is broken, ugly, and dead, and it stinks. What does the Bible say about people who are all froth and no substance? God calls their bluff when His prophet wrote, "The wicked *are* like the troubled sea, when it cannot rest, whose waters cast up mire and dirt. *There is* no peace," says my God, "for the wicked" (Isaiah 57:20–21). By living a double life, children who are spiritual hypocrites struggle to keep up appearances. Because he/she is all show and no substance and all "foam" and no faithfulness, the child who is like "the wave of the sea [that is] driven and tossed" (see James 1:6, Ephesians 4:14) by the values of society, will find no spiritual rest—except in a close salvation relationship with Jesus Christ. Parents have a God-given right to examine the faith of their children. Examine their spiritual substance often. Know the difference between fruit and foliage. Help your children grow in their relationship with Jesus Christ as they "work out what Christ works in."

14. Without repentance, their path will never lead them any closer to a fulfilling (spiritually satisfying) relationship with Christ. (Jude 13). As Jude states, they are like wandering stars (planets) who are doomed to experience a "roaming existence" in spiritual darkness that will never draw them closer to the S-o-n (Jesus) unless they repent of their sins, change the course of their lives, and set the commitments of their hearts on Christ.

So what can children do to keep themselves from the "apostrophe" and/or "apostasy" of a relationship that has drifted away from Christ?

Jude 17–23. What children can do to keep themselves from "turning aside" or from "turning away" from the faith

1. Jude 17. Remember God's words. Learn them. Apply them. Obey them.
2. Jude 20–21. Remain in God's way—practice spiritual faithfulness. Even though no one can "see" faith, everyone can notice the footprints of faithfulness. In living your life, leave behind some faithful footprints for Christ.
3. Jude 22–23. Live outside of yourself by reaching out to others with the compassion of Jesus Christ, which is a love that cannot be restrained no matter what the cost (Jude 22–23). Choose a life of gratefulness that resembles the character qualities of the One who gave His life to save your soul.

Key questions (from Genesis 4:1–7 and Jude):[16]

Were Cain or Abel nurtured in vain? Were Adam and Eve good parents—in society's eyes? Were they good parents—in God's eyes? Today, can children be nurtured in vain? Choose one: Is parenting a futile endeavor? Is it a rewarding and fulfilling experience? Or is it both? In your opinion, did Adam and Eve name their second child based on the impressions and disappointments resulting from the raising of their first child, Cain?[17] Knowing that every child of God is "accepted in the Beloved [One] (Jesus)" (see Ephesians 1:6), do all children have the potential to live a life that pleases God and fulfils His plan? Living a life that reflects the child's love for Jesus, can every child overcome human expectations and live a life that God will bless? If a family's first child does not live up to the parents' exalted expectations of being a doctor, a lawyer, or "someone successful in society," should parents expect the next child(ren) to exceed the expectations of the first?[18] Of the two sons of history's first parents, which is remembered more: The one who expected God to honor the work of his hands or the son who trusted God to honor the worship of his heart? (Abel still speaks: Hebrews 11:4.) From Jude, define "the way of Cain" (see Jude 11; 2 Timothy 4:3–4; Hebrews 11:4; 1 John 3:12, 15). See the author's content on 2 Timothy 4:3–4. In a matter that relates to child-rearing and the future lives of your children, define and discuss the following terms: "apostrophe" ("a turning away") and a "[walking toward] apostasy" ("a turning aside"). From Jude 4–13, since many parents experience the heartache of having a child "turn away from" or "turn aside from" the truth, what characterizes children who defect, depart, disappear, leave, or fall away from their faith? How many of these characteristics are found in your child(ren)? From Jude 17–23, what can children do to keep themselves from the "apostrophe" and/or "apostasy" of a relationship that has drifted away from Christ?

History's Second Abel

Ecclesiastes 1:2; Selected Passages from Proverbs
("Parenting by the Book: Principles from Proverbs")

THREE THOUSAND AND TWENTY-SIX YEARS after the death of Adam and Eve's Abel,[19] a man with seven hundred wives, three hundred concubines, and many other (international) lovers[20] potentially had more children than the offspring that scripture mentions by name: Solomon's son, Rehoboam, of 1 Kings 11:43; and Solomon's two daughters, Taphath of 1 Kings 4:11 and Basmath of 1 Kings 4:15.[21] Given wisdom as a gift of insight and discernment from God,[22] whether he had three children or hundreds, the husband and father Solomon should have known how to raise his offspring for the Lord. He had the best teacher: God. Yet, because he allowed himself to be influenced by society's values, worldly advice, the opinions of well-meaning contemporaries, and the child-rearing philosophies of people who rejected any relationship of commitment with Solomon's God, Solomon failed to apply God's wisdom to a parent's most important task: raising his offspring in the fear and admonition (training and instruction) of the Lord (see Ephesians 6:4).[23] In writing one of his two books that exist unto this day, Solomon looked back on his life's compromises, on his failure to surrender his most important commitments to God, and on those many occasions when Solomon treated the God of the Bible as merely one of many "equal-in-authority" gods, Solomon used the name of Adam and Eve's second son as the theme of Ecclesiastes. He wrote, "Abel of Abels," [says] the preacher. "Abel of Abels. All is Abel (vanity/emptiness/futility)" (Ecclesiastes 1:2). Solomon's use of the Hebrew word *Abel* implies that Ecclesiastes is a lamentation describing both Solomon's and society's failure to fear (respect) God and keep His commandments (see Ecclesiastes 12:13).[24] Thankfully Solomon would write another book that gives all parents today an opportunity to "not repeat" Solomon's mistakes. It is the book of Proverbs, which includes "child-raising" passages that help modern-day dads and moms "parent by the Book." In discovering the references where the terms *son, sons, son's, daughter, child, children, children's, father, mother, father's, mother's, generation,* and *generations* occur, the passages from Proverbs are as follows:[25]

Proverbs 1:1–4. There are reasons why God gave children parents.

> The proverbs of Solomon the son of David, king of Israel; To know wisdom and instruction; to perceive the words of understanding; To receive the instruction of wisdom, justice, and judgment, and equity; To give subtilty to the simple, to the young man knowledge and discretion. (Proverbs 1:1–4)

From his experience as David's favorite son, Solomon understood the underlying purposes of parenting. Although he could have spoken from the perspective of a son, Solomon the father listed ten reasons why God gave children parents. What are ten God-given responsibilities that parents have when raising their children for the Lord? As disciplers for Jesus Christ, parents must teach their children the following:

1. "To know [biblical] wisdom" (Proverbs 1:2), which is uncommon sense in an uncommon degree (1 Kings 3:16–28); biblical discernment (Matthew 16:3), the ability to make choices approved by God (Proverbs 5:1); and "the God-given ability to make God-informed and God-centered decisions in life" (James 1:5–6). When Paul shared wisdom, he wrote, "Be careful for nothing; but in everything by prayer and supplication with thanksgiving let your requests be made known unto God; and the peace of God which passes all understanding will keep your hearts and minds through Christ Jesus" (Philippians 4:6–7). God's wisdom puts God's will in focus. In using this term *wisdom* in other Old Testament passages, the wisdom that "is from above" (James 3:13) allows the believer to combine the discernment of a seamstress as she sews together a garment (Exodus 28:3), the technical skills of a craftsman as he puts together a building (Exodus 35:10), the management skills of a government official (1 Kings 5:21), and the counseling skills of one who handles a delicate matter (2 Samuel 14:2) to disciple and influence his/her child to see life from God's perspective and live that life in a manner that pleases the greatest Father of all: God. Of all the biblical qualities that parents should teach and, of all the scriptural commodities that children should pursue, "Wisdom *is* the principal thing; *therefore* get wisdom" (Proverbs 4:7). May each parent make sure that his/her children drinks often from the well of the wisdom of God. Read Bible stories to your children. Discuss scripture. Take your children to church. Expose your children to "age-appropriate" Bible ministries (through various media providers—online, the radio, social media, television, bookstores, children's Bible studies, local ministries, Christian schools, and others). Lead your children to Christ at the earliest possible age. Disciple your children. Pray with them. Expose them to missions. Tell them your "story" concerning your spiritual

growth. With them, share your testimony of faith. Discuss biblical (God-centered) goals for life. Talk to them about God around your dinner table. Invest time in their spiritual life. Teach them to trust. Help them through trials. Recognize that no believer is perfect—all will fail occasionally. Lift them up. Help them to stand. And, since everyone is either a missionary or a mission field, encourage your children to share their faith in Christ. Teach them "what is wisdom."

2. "To know [biblical] instruction" (Proverbs 1:2), which is "discipline through teaching." Instruction is the parents' means to help their children distinguish truth from error and positive behavior from negative behavior. It is the "disciplines of the Christian life." Without the time investment of instruction, children will not develop the skills necessary to cope with life. Yet, far too often, parents delegate the majority of this responsibility to others—outside the home. Since, as the "prince of this world," Satan has no desire to encourage any believer's spiritual growth or development toward God (see John 14:30, Ephesians 2:2, 2 Corinthians 4:4), is society interested in helping you parent your child for Christ? No. So do not seek society's favor. Will the school bring to life what the home puts to death? Rarely. If parents want their children to find a Father in God, they need to find something of God in their father. What is the means of accomplishing biblical instruction? In comparing scripture with scripture, the Bible gives insight concerning that answer. In Deuteronomy 11:2 the term *instruction* is translated "punishment" or "chastisement" and makes reference to the chastening of physical correction. In Hosea 5:2 the term "*instruction*" speaks of "[verbal] rebuke, spoken counsel" and of "making something right." Solomon combined both methods in Proverbs 29:15 when he mentioned the "rod" of physical correction (spanking) in the same breath as the spoken word of verbal counsel/rebuke. In other words, be balanced biblically when you practice healthy discipline on behalf of your child. In combination, both physical correction and verbal rebuke are needed to help children discover God's wisdom for life. Biblically, use both.

3. "To perceive the words of understanding" (Proverbs 1:2), which speaks of "the ability to discern the difference" between spoken insights that are inconsistent with scripture and biblically consistent verbal directions that guide the parents' children into a God-focused perspective on how to live a God-honoring life that results in the mature child becoming a person of character in a world of compromise.[26] To know what society teaches is common. Parents are inundated with secular philosophies, clamoring voices that promote society's system of values, humanistic methodologies, and "how to parent" programs that remove God from the parenting equation and Christ from the consciousness of your child. To know what God knows—but what society does not know—is the result of biblical parenting. A child should never stop learning about God and His Word. In parenting by the Book,

encourage your children to maintain a consciousness of God continually. Understand this: your children do not belong to the world. Your children belong to God.

4. "To receive the instruction of wisdom" (Proverbs 1:3). To "receive," as in John 1:12, means to "warmly welcome" (someone or something) or invite "someone or something" in ("make it your own"). It is the same action as plucking or taking grapes. *Receive* is the term "taken" in Genesis 2:22 where the Lord took a rib out of Adam's side and made a woman. If wisdom is pictured as a woman (see Proverbs 1:20–33 and Proverbs 8–9), then she should be "warmly welcomed" (invited in), by your children, so that her instruction in biblical disciplines can be heard (see the term *instruction* in Proverbs 1:2). Children have a difficult time looking beyond the surface. Teach them to see in layers and to look beyond the obvious. Educate them on how to use and apply wisdom. Like a quality chess player, have them think beyond life's first moves. Just as a highway has curves around which a traveler cannot see, so does the journey of life. To an infant, a polished quarter is more appealing than a $100 bill. Yet the paper bill is far more valuable. In life, just as in a store, there is a difference between "values" and "price tags." Teach your children that "all that glitters is not gold." What your child cannot see underneath the surface may be harmful to his/her physical and/or spiritual and emotional health. Until your children learn to think on their own, think for them. Then, while discussing the processes of thought with them, encourage them to think biblically on their own. Help them to see beyond the obvious to what is really there. Teach them how to use the wisdom that the parents model in the home.

5. "To receive the instruction of justice" (Proverbs 1:3). Since "instruction" is discipline gained through two forms of teaching (physical correction and verbal counsel/rebuke), what is the direction of that instruction? The goal is "justice," which is "righteousness" (something that is straight/walking straight spiritually). Children are both curious and easily led astray. When departing from God's truth, they leave the straight paths illumined by God's light to walk in the ways of darkness (Proverbs 2:13). God wants His children to carefully walk in God's straight path, pondering all their ways (Proverbs 4:26). That is why parents need to say continually, "This is the way, you walk in it" (Isaiah 30:21). Enforce the "principle of a godly walk." Make it a well-worn path. Celebrate with them when your children walk the path of faith. Be an example and walk that straight pathway yourself.

6. "To receive the instruction of judgment" (Proverbs 1:3). In addition to wisdom and righteousness, children must "pluck off" (the Hebrew word for this term "receive"—*la-qua-hat*—is a grape-harvester's term for plucking a grape off of a vine) from the family's tree good judgment, which is the ability to manage the affairs of others (Judges 8:20), to determine truth when faced with contradictory reports (Psalm 72:2–4), and to put good decisions into practice (1 Samuel 24:15). When people question a child's judgment, if that child's judgment matches God's good judgment from scripture, then, when that child faces situations in his/

her home, circumstances at work, difficulties in relationships, or conflicting choices, that child—as an adult—will be able to pluck from the available choice list right decisions and make those biblically consistent decisions without the parents' immediate help. Instructing your child in "judgment" prepares your child to live on his/her own—later in life—and to make his/her own decisions in a manner consistent with the guidance given by God. Knowing that children will "leave the nest" eventually, we raise our children to live apart from us—later in life—in their own established homes. Get them off the screen. Get them into the book that teaches them wisdom: God's Word. No matter the source, there is no better advice for your children than what they will receive from God's Word. Immerse them in the Word and, properly applied, your children will live pure and clean lives that are set apart from sin—both now and in the future. By acting on the Word that your children have been taught, your offspring can put good decisions into practice and continue to make right choices when confronted with the circumstances of life.

7. "To receive wisdom in equity" (Proverbs 1:3). Every parent wants to remove certain obstacles in the emotional, spiritual, intellectual, medical, or geographical pathway that the parent's child will travel. From the parent's knowledge and lifetime of experience in sharing "wisdom in equity," the parent gives the child the ability to make God-informed and God-centered decisions in life so that the child knows how to go straight as the parent removes obstacles from the child's pathway. Of the coming of John the Baptist, who served to remove obstacles from the pathway of Jesus so that He could get to people and so people could get to Him, a Bible prophet used the term *equity* when he wrote, "The voice of one crying in the wilderness: 'Prepare the way of the Lord; make straight (remove the obstacles), in the desert, a highway for our God" (Isaiah 40:3). That's not all. In addition to making something straight by removing the obvious obstacles, the term *equity* is used also of the words and ways of God, which are always upright and always fair. Fair, fair! What is fair? Balanced responses are fair. Biblical parents teach their children to weigh everything in the balance (Psalm 58:1) by seeking to level out each side's argument so that decisions are based on facts and not on emotions, which tend to cloud judgment when conclusions are made. We told our children often to "be character driven, not emotion led." That is good advice for all as we encourage our children to seek fairness ("equity"), without prejudice.

8. "To give prudence to the simple" (Proverbs 1:4). Often Bible words are taken from the culture. *Prudence* is the word the seamstress used to describe material that had no folds or pleats. It is the "subtilty" of Proverbs 12:2, the "guile" of Exodus 21:14, and the "craftiness" of Job 5:13. In the context of family life, it is the parent treating the child as new material that has not yet been shaped or patterned by the world. When they are born, children are "simple." Equated with Solomon's proverbial fool, they love simplicity (Proverbs 1:22), are devoid of deeper understanding (Proverbs 7:7), are gullible (Proverbs 9:4, 16; 14:15), and

turn away from wisdom (Proverbs 1:32). Left to their own devices, all children are destined for folly (Proverbs 14:18, 24). Yet godly parents intervene and break this cycle of mediocrity so that each child can live a God-shaped and Christ-centered life. Must children live in sin to know what sin is like? No! If a brand new piece of paper is folded over and creased, it shows the folds. Before it was creased and folded, it was a smooth piece of paper. But creased and folded, it is crumpled and out of shape. Before society's values get ahold of your child's heart, folding it, creasing it, and using it up through sin—like the seamstress of Proverbs 1:4—parents need to share "prudence" when the child is young and unfolded and without wrinkles so the child might grow to walk in wisdom before he/she is old enough to make the choice to rebel. Refuse to let society fold and crease your child into its mold. Your child does not fit society's pattern or its value's mold! Into the fabric of your child, weave the crimson thread that runs from cover to cover through scripture—the redemptive love, grace, and teachings of Jesus Christ. In intervening against society as it seeks to shape the material—which is your child—into its pattern, refuse society's advances by influencing your child to keep the shape God intended for him/her to have.

9. "To [give] the young man knowledge" (Proverbs 1:4). In scripture, a "young man" can be anyone between birth and marriage (Proverbs 22:6). In contrast to knowledge gained by education, the knowledge of Proverbs 1:4 is information gained by the experiences of others (Proverbs 2:5–10). Parents were not born yesterday. Since each parent has a history of lessons learned from the parent's own valuable life experiences, children are not required to learn every life lesson from their own experience. Parents can share testimonies from their own experiences, and from the lives of personalities in scripture, so that their children can learn from their parents and from scripture's personalities as each child grows in the "grace and knowledge" of our Lord and Savior Jesus Christ (2 Peter 3:18).[27] Be imaginative. As your children write their own personal stories, open your diary—from life—and, with discernment and balanced discretion, share your life-experience stories with them. Then, as your children write their stories one line and chapter at a time, encourage them to learn from your victories and from your mistakes. In a sense, share with your child your personal "memoirs" from life—both the good and the bad, with discretion—so that your child can learn from them.

10. "To [give] the young man discretion" (Proverbs 1:4), which is a "godly purpose" for life and living (Proverbs 2:11). Parents need to help their children think beyond the surface level, be alert, and live cautiously so that each child can avoid dangerous tendencies in life. Among other material, what sources of information should parents share with their children in order to keep their children from the emotional, intellectual, and societal influences that might confuse them or cause them to make decisions inconsistent with God's will, purpose, and ways? Should parents allow other children, other children's parents, or other

outside influences such as secular philosophers or the media to usurp the parents' God-given function to be your child's #1 influence in life?[28] The term translated "discretion" in Proverbs 1:4 is similar, like a cousin, to the term translated "psalms" in the hymn book of the Jews. Since, in the Psalms, David and others disclosed the circumstances and revealed the experiences that taught them discretion, when you have devotions with your children, spend some time in the Psalms.[29] When you do, in helping your children to know what God says their purpose is, God's words will be like "goads"—given by [God's] Shepherd to keep your children going in the right direction (Ecclesiastes 12:11). Allow your children to enter life through the doorway of scripture—and the parents' God-directed experiences—and your children will be kept from much of the evil that society intends for them.

Proverbs 1:7–9. Teach your children respect for authority in the home, and they will respect authority when they are outside the home.

> The fear of the LORD is the beginning of knowledge, but fools despise wisdom and instruction. My son, hear the instruction of your father, and do not forsake (leave fallow or to leave unplowed) the law (teaching) of your mother: For they will be a graceful ornament on your head, and chains about your neck. (Proverbs 1:7–9)

Biblical "fear" makes reference to a healthy dose of respect and the ability to take God seriously.[30] When raising your child, since biblical "fear" is the "beginning" (starting place) of/for wisdom, start there by teaching your child, from the earliest age, to take God seriously. The further society is removed from the era of respect for God, the further removed are the family's children from respect for their parents. The term "Lord," in Proverbs 1:7, is "Jehovah," which is the name for the "God to Whom we give an account." Whether acknowledged or not, every person who ever lived will stand before God one day and answer for his/her response to God's authority—whether as a believer at the Bema Seat of Christ (see 2 Corinthians 5:10–11 and Romans 14:10–12) or as an unbeliever at the Great White Throne judgment (see Revelation 20:7–15). "Wisdom" is the ability to make God-informed and God-centered decisions in life (see James 1:5–8; 3:13). Is your child wise or otherwise? "Instruction" is discipline through teaching and the parents' means to help their children distinguish truth from error and good behavior from bad behavior. Does your child behave what he/she believes? Solomon was direct. Knowing that if a child does not start with a respect for authority in the home the child does not start at all, Solomon's first lesson (starting point on the child's pathway to life) for his wayward son Rehoboam was, "respect the God to Whom you will give an account." As taught in Proverbs 1:7b, a person is a "fool" to live as if God does not exist—to live without God in this world.[31] Yet lessons on godly respect are lessons often neglected. To encourage respect (see Proverbs 1:8), a primary goal in parenting must be the giving of "instruction" (which is the same term Solomon used in Proverbs 1:3). The knowledge of God does not come naturally. Knowing that the lifelong welfare of every child is directly related to the response each child has to the parents' authority in the home (in this passage: to the "father's" authority in the home), if children are to acquire the knowledge of the enablement, empowerment, and companionship of the God to Whom we must give an account, fathers must teach their children of "Jehovah God" (the Lord) and to heed His words. One obvious way to teach this spiritual discipline is for fathers to teach respect for parental authority and to have a testimony that deserves the child's respect.[32] Knowing that Jewish children had the first five books of the Old Testament (commonly called the Books of the Law) memorized by the time they were five years old (verse by verse—every verse), "mothers" must teach their children the scriptures.[33] As implied by the Hebrew term *forsake*, mothers must teach in a manner similar to a farmer sowing seed. They must make sure the "seed of instruction" does not remain "fallow" but instead takes root in the soil of their child's heart. When knowledge, wisdom, instruction, and God's Word do take root in the child's heart, God's favor—on that child's life—is as obvious as a "headdress/ornament" worn on a head and a necklace (pendant) worn around a neck. The initial recipient of Solomon's Book of Proverbs was Solomon's wayward son Rehoboam. Most parents blame their children when their children go astray ("We couldn't do anything with them," or "It's not our fault that our children turned out this way"). Because Solomon did not practice what he presented in Proverbs, Rehoboam had a fool for a dad who compromised every principle of wisdom possible and, by example, passed his lack of respect for (God's) authority on to his son. Since Rehoboam's mother was an idol-worshipping Ammonitess who did not believe in God, Rehoboam did not hear many of God's truths when taught on his mother's knee. Instead unbelief and a lack of respect for Jehovah was modeled and taught, by his mother, in his home. By the time children are full-grown, parents can try to undo their child-rearing mistakes "until the cows come home," but, without an intervention by the Holy Spirit of God, the parents will have raised a generation of fools.

Proverbs 1:10–16. Because peer groups can influence your child to engage in spiritually negative activities and live a life that does not please God, parents must monitor their child(ren)'s peer groups.

> My son, if sinners entice you, do not consent. If they say, "Come with us, let us lie in wait to shed blood; let us lurk secretly for the innocent without cause; Let us swallow them alive like Sheol (the grave); and whole, like those who go down to the Pit; We shall find all kinds of precious possessions, we shall fill our houses with spoil: Cast in your lot among us; let us all have one purse: My son, do not walk in the way with them, keep (refrain) your foot from their path; For their feet run to evil, and they make haste (are quick) to shed blood. (Proverbs 1:10–16)

Just as children should respect authority (Proverbs 1:7–9), children should remain pure in their behaviors (Proverbs 1:10–17). Just as full-grown adults rejected God's authority and said, "Let us … Let us … Let us" in Genesis 11:3, 4a, 4b[34] (in the context of the building of the Tower of

Babel), Rehoboam's acquaintances used the same terminology when the "let us" pressure/influence of his peers invited Solomon's son to participate in violent gang activity (in Proverbs 1:11), take advantage of the weak (in Proverbs 1:12), and live outside the lines (defy authority) for profit (in Proverbs 1:13–14). Perhaps Solomon's counsel to his son Rehoboam came "too little, too late" to resist temptations presented by peers, to run from evil, to avoid the snares of Satan, and to live in God's light instead of the devil's darkness (see Proverbs 1:15–16). Sin requires no incubation period. Its first occurrence is often full-blown. Unless children can "fly like a bird" above sin's snares, it is easy to get caught—whether willingly or unwittingly—in activities involving sin. In using the same terminology as the tempters did in Proverbs 1:11, 12, and 14, God used the phrase "let us" to invite His children to participate in activities that honor His truths when He said, "Let us draw near with a true heart in full assurance of faith (develop a close relationship with God) … Let us hold fast the confession of *our* hope without wavering (keep your "Christ commitments" current for the Lord) … And let us consider one another in order to stir up love and good works (be aware that others are watching to see how committed you are to the Lord" (Hebrews 10:22–25). In which "let us" patch will you live—the one that leads to sin or the one that is blessed by God?

Proverbs 2:1–5. Concerning parental instruction, receptive children are blessed children. What children do with God's Word when they are young will determine the direction of their lives.

> My son, if you receive my words, and treasure my commands within you, So that you incline your ear to wisdom, *and* apply your heart to understanding; Yes, if you cry out for discernment, *and* lift up your voice for understanding, If you seek her as silver, and search for her as *for* hidden treasures; Then you will understand the fear of the Lord, and find the knowledge of God. (Proverbs 2:1–5)

To "receive" means to "welcome something/someone warmly as if an old friend has come to visit." Wise children warmly welcome the godly counsel of their parents, knowing it will result in the blessings of the Lord (see the term *receive* in Proverbs 1:3). To "incline your ear" is to "lay something on the ground like a blanket." It is to "make your ear attentive—to have your spiritual hearing aids on." Wise children "lay out" their mind's receptors "like a blanket" so that God can fill them with His truth (see Nehemiah 9:34 where Israel's kings and princes refused to "lay out their ears" or "pay attention to" God's laws and His commandments).[35] To "treasure" is to "store something up that is precious." What is more precious than the life-sustaining truths of God (see Proverbs 2:1, Psalm 119:11)? To "cry out" is to "aggressively plead and call/summon someone to come and help." Children need to do more than give "lip service" to a pursuit of discernment. They need to passionately seek wisdom from the God Who promises to give it liberally and withhold it not, when we ask Him for it (see the phrase "cry out" in Proverbs 2:3 and James 1:5–8). To "seek" is to "aggressively pursue something or someone." Since wisdom is presented as a woman (see Proverbs 1:20–33 and Proverbs

8–9), wisdom is a "person" whom every child should pursue. If a child's success in life was based on his/her current knowledge of and pursuit of the truths of God, how successful would that child be? Since God's estimation of success is based on the knowledge of God's Word and its application into life, what should parents counsel their children to do in order for their children to obtain the knowledge and wisdom that will help them live their lives in a manner that honors the Lord (see also Joshua 1:6–8)? Here are three recommendations given by Solomon to his son (these are recommendations that every child would be wise to pursue):

1. Be receptive to God's Word (Proverbs 2:1). In introducing this section with the term "if," Solomon implied that people have a choice, in their pursuit of or neglect of God's truth—to apply it or avoid it. What children do with God's Word will determine the direction and destiny of their lives. Have an inquisitive attitude toward God's Word. Be interested enough in God's Word to let it have a recognized presence in your life.
2. Willingly respond, in positive ways, to God's Word (Proverbs 2:2–4). Children who respect God's Word as their final authority will incline, apply, cry out, lift up their voice, and seek God's Word as people search for valuable hidden treasure. Perhaps Solomon acquired this concept of treating God's Word as a priceless treasure when David wrote, "Your word I have hidden ("treasured up and stored") in my heart, that I might not sin against You" (Psalm 119:11). Love God's Word enough to live it.
3. Like a miner looking for precious metals, be resolved to find (discover) the truths of God's Word (Proverbs 2:5). Mining for precious metals requires committed determination and dedicated work to dig it out of the ground. As with mining silver or gold, digging into God's Word to discover God's truths takes time. As a child of the King, pursue God's riches with the same energy as others pursue other forms of wealth (see Luke 15:8–10 where the woman sought diligently for her lost coin). Treat God's Word as precious. It will bless your life.

Proverbs 3:1–6. Because children need direction on their journey through life, children must trust God's guidebook: His Word (the Bible).

> My son, do not forget my law, but let your heart keep my commands; For length of days and long life and peace they will add to you. Let not mercy and truth forsake you; bind them around your neck, write them on the tablet of your heart, *and* so find favor and high esteem in the sight of God and man. Trust in the LORD with all your heart, and lean not on your own understanding; In all your ways acknowledge Him, and He shall direct your paths. (Proverbs 3:1–6)

In the progression of the book of Proverbs, Solomon spoke as a spiritual father to a foolish son. It is one thing for a child to have head knowledge of God's commands, which are what God wants for our lives. It is another thing for a child to allow God's commands to become such a part of his/her life that life's natural response is obedience to the Lord (Proverbs 3:1). What is the result of "owning obedience" and of loving God and His Word so much that the child obeys God's commands?[36] Children will be kept from sin's dangerous invasions and be rewarded with long life that is good (see Exodus 20:12, Ephesians 6:2). Place a high value on obedience to God, and God will "lengthen your days" (which refers to the quality of your life)[37] and "add to your life" (which refers to the quantity of years in your life). In addition, Solomon implored his son to make sure that God's Word had an ever-present place in his life. Instead of allowing God's merciful loving-kindness[38] and His truth to be forsaken (literally: "left behind" or "left out" of Rehoboam's life),[39] Solomon said that his son Rehoboam should do more than treasure up God's Word in his heart. As a child, he should bring it with him daily, in a tangible way, as a constant reminder of Who is in charge of Rehoboam's life (Proverbs 3:4). How is this accomplished? In modern times, children can carry a hard-copy of God's Word or bring with them digital access to the scriptures on a tablet or on some other electronic device. In Solomon's day, both children and adults carried with them phylacteries, which were leather pouches or cloth bags in which believers would place passages of scripture (the most common scripture passages carried in Solomon's day were Exodus 13:1–10, 11–16, and 20–23 and Deuteronomy 6:4–9, 11:13–21).[40] The best way to allow God's Word to have a constant presence in a person's life is to memorize scripture and then apply that scripture to daily life. When a child merely has the head knowledge of scripture, that child will obey God because he/she "ought to" or "has to." But when God's Word takes up residence in the child's heart, the child will say, "I want to" and then will obey. Hearing it, the child will heed God's Word and be respected by both God and man (Proverbs 3:1, 4). Then, in a classic passage of scripture that provides a road map for living, Solomon gave children three recommendations on how to live their lives:[41]

1. "Trust in the Lord with all your heart" (Proverbs 3:5). Rely on God. *Trust* is from a root word that speaks of a rope that is stretched out taut. It pictures a God follower on his journey through life, coming to a crossroads, throwing himself/herself down on the ground, and lying there extended on the dirt casting all of his/her hopes for the present and the future on someone else: God. It is a person attaching the rope of his/her life to the throne of God and shortening the rope. Who is a child to trust? Certainly children should trust believing parents. But only God can apply His full array of attributes to overcome and provide in every situation. His perfect love, balanced by His perfect holiness, guarantees that God will never let us go and never let us down. What is a believer to do? Trust. Who is to trust? Four times in two verses, Solomon used the word *your* as in "your heart … your understanding … your ways … your paths." People on life's journey—that is you and that is me—need to "rely on/ trust" God for guidance. How should believers trust? With all our hearts, souls, and minds (see Matthew 22:37, Mark 12:30–31, Luke 10:27, Deuteronomy 6:5). The flawed faith of a

divided heart and a double-mind is no trust at all. Since "all means all and that's all that all can mean," God expects a heart that is, without reservation, totally surrendered to "trust" during all the circumstances of life. Perhaps that is why Solomon wrote, "He who trusts in his own heart is a fool" (Proverbs 28:26). "Love God, trust God." "Love self, trust self." In the toughest of times, Job commented, "Though He slay me, yet will I trust in Him" (Job 13:15). Be committed to trusting God. When you trust the results to God, He will work it out in the life of your child.

2. "Lean not on your own understanding" (Proverbs 3:5). Rest the entire weight and direction of your decisions/choices on God. As the first term in the word order in the original Hebrew text, "understanding" is the emphasis of the passage. Coupled with the term *lean* (the Hebrew term *ti-say-en*), which makes reference to a shepherd's staff that is given for stability, support, assistance, and protection, the phrase "lean not on your own understanding" makes it clear that children should not seek to cope with life on their own. If they do, they are like the Philistine's pillars in the days of Samson that fell when an outside influence (Samson's strength) toppled them (Judges 16:26). In addition they are like Saul's spear on which the king leaned as his source of strength, instead of on God (see 2 Samuel 1:12). In contrast, on the banks of the Red Sea, although Moses was advised by some to run, he took the advice of God to "stand still and see the salvation of the Lord" (Exodus 14:13). As a result, the nation, through whom Christ would come, was saved because Moses raised his staff while "leaning on God." Anxious moms, frustrated dads, and concerned children need to understand that God delivers in His own ways. In life, if you want to be emotionally drained, scheme your way through life by coping with circumstances on your own. If you want to experience God's peace and rest, release the decisions of your life to Him.

3. "In all your ways acknowledge Him and He will direct your paths" (Proverbs 3:6). If you have a personal relationship with God, own it and acknowledge it. The phrase "in all your ways" makes reference to "every decision in life." A second term: "Acknowledge" is a word that means "remember." When faced with life's decisions, believing parents need to remember that they have something that unbelievers lack: a personal "salvation-relationship" with Christ that includes the guidance and direction of God's indwelling Holy Spirit (see 1 Corinthians 2:9–16). As a result, as people do with other people with whom they have relationships, parents need to talk to God in prayer, open God's guidebook on child-rearing (the Bible), and consult the architect of every family that ever existed on earth.[42] Seek God's counsel through prayer and His Word, and God will direct your paths or smooth out and remove the obstacles in your pathway that keep you from making wise decisions in life. When remembering that you have a personal relationship with God, He will clear away your confusion, direct you into His perfect will, and make your way straight. Therefore, concerning your children, rely on God; rest the entire weight of your decisions on Him, and

remember that He has a presence in your life. When facing difficulties, remember also the truth of Romans 8:28, "[That] we know that all things work together for good to those who love God, to those who are the called according to *His* purpose." Even on those occasions where it is not clear whether or not what is happening to you is God's will, acknowledge this: God's will or not, God allowed it. In the midst of God's will, the believer must see the "Who" in what is happening as well as the "what." When focusing on the "what," believers must understand that the last phrase in Romans 8:28 is not "His will" but instead "His purpose," which means that, one day, God will reveal the "why" of every circumstance. In the meantime, trust the "what" to Him.

Proverbs 3:11–12. Children must not waste the parental discipline they receive when they are young.

> My son, do not despise the chastening of the LORD, nor detest His correction; For whom the LORD loves He corrects, just as a father the son *in whom* he delights." (Proverbs 3:11–12)

"Correction" is discipline and training. Although correction is necessary in the life of every child, the father who seeks to discover God the Father's reflection in the life of his children needs to understand that even biblical correction can have one of two results:

1. The child can learn from his/her correction and receive the "peaceable fruit" of what is right in life (Hebrews 12:11).
2. Children can "despise" and "detest" their correction (Proverbs 3:11).

The term *detest* means "to loathe." The term *despise* was a household term. It was used of "something wasted or refused" like the family's trash (see Lamentations 3:45). Israel "despised" (rejected) God's counsel and, like grown children who—looking back—rejected the godly counsel of their believing parents, could not find their way and wandered in a wilderness for [thirty-eight to forty] years (see Psalm 78:40–66; Acts 7:37–43, 13:17–18). When Israel "trashed" and rejected God's plan that God rule Israel, God's children demanded another authority to lead them. God granted their request and gave them Saul before He gave them David (1 Samuel 8:7, 10:17–25). As God did with Israel on their exodus journey, the nation's rejection of God's will brought leanness to their bones (Psalm 106:15). In Amos 2:4 and Isaiah 5:25, God's children rejected the Word of the Lord, treated scripture like trash, and cast it aside (threw it out) like garbage. The result was a groping in spiritual darkness when they could have walked in God's light. In Psalm 118:22, God's people rejected the stone that was to become the headstone for the temple's corner. It took God's children years to find it. Modern-day children who reject God's will and ways serve themselves and, wandering aimlessly—with little purpose, waste many years that God could bless. The hand of parental discipline is a valuable character developer that should be cherished. Yet, when rejected or detested (loathed), a child's future is limited to self-produced blessings. Respond to the nail-pierced hand of Jesus. He holds a cross, not a rod. Allow Jesus to guide your child's life and his/her blessings will be limited only by the resources of grace that God is willing to share.

Proverbs 3:21–26. Often the bad decisions a child makes when he/she is young become stumbling blocks to the child's future success in life.

My son, let them not depart from your eyes—keep sound wisdom and discretion; So they will be life to your soul and grace to your neck. Then you will walk safely in your way, and your foot will not stumble. When you lie down, you will not be afraid; Yes, you will lie down and your sleep will be sweet. Do not be afraid of sudden terror, nor of trouble from the wicked when it comes; For the Lord will be your confidence, and will keep your foot from being caught." (Proverbs 3:21–26)

Older people stumble. Younger people know the confidence of stability. Yet Solomon spoke of feet that stumble (Proverbs 3:23) and get caught (Proverbs 3:26). As a hiker, I know that one misstep or one oddly placed tree root can cause my feet to stumble and impact negatively the rest of the hike. This is true also of bad or reckless decisions that a child makes when he/she is young—especially during the middle school or high school years. Persuaded by the crowd to dishonor Christ, a child can suffer for life—long after the "crowd" has moved on, picked up with a different crowd of followers, and/or vanished away. As your children journey through life, God wants to give them stability. As they close their eyes to sleep, the God Who never sleeps wants to give them protection (see Psalm 121:4). Yet wrong decisions—made when children are young—can negatively limit what God wants to do in your children's lives. Point them toward Christ. Make a life of conformity to Christ the goal and direction of each child's life.[43] Choose wisely. Be careful when making decisions. Choices that are inconsistent with scripture can lead to a life filled with regrets.

Proverbs 4:1–9: Just as parents have a responsibility to instruct their children in matters pertaining to biblical wisdom and godly understanding, children have a responsibility to both receive the parents' teachings when they are children and retain the parents' instruction for the rest of their lives.

Hear, *my* children, the instruction of a father, and give attention to know understanding; For I give you good doctrine: do not forsake my law. When I was my father's son, tender and the only one in the sight of my mother, He also taught me, and said to me: "Let your heart retain my words; keep my commands, and live. Get wisdom! Get understanding! Do not forget, nor turn away from the words of my mouth. Do not forsake her, and she will preserve you; Love her, and she will keep you. Wisdom *is* the principal thing; *therefore* get wisdom. And in all your getting, get understanding. Exalt her, and she will promote you; she will bring you honor, when you embrace her. She will place on your head an ornament of grace; a crown of glory she will deliver to you. (Proverbs 4:1–9)

In introducing this text, Solomon instructed his son (Proverbs 4:1–2), looked back and recognized the teachings that Solomon received from his father David (Proverbs 4:3–4), and then instructed his son again (Proverbs 4:5–9). In the cycle of life, parents do give good advice. I wonder if Solomon, when he was a child, ever thought that he would be giving instructions to his own son one day—the same instructions that he received from his father David.[44] The term "hear" means to "heed" as well as to "listen." "Instruction" is verbal counsel. In the Hebrew, "father" can refer to a biological father, father who adopts a grandfather, a caregiver, or someone else whom the child respects. In this case, the father is Solomon. "Give attention to" speaks of listening with "both ears on." To "know" is to "gain" or "become known by" the teachings a child has received (the obedient application of biblical instruction, received in the home, will identify the child as a "practicing believer" who actively follows Christ). "Doctrine" is teachings. To "forsake" means to "abandon" or to "leave something behind." How often do children, when they are grown, seek their own way and leave behind the teachings of their parents? I've often wondered how difficult it is for grown children who have forsaken the teachings of their parents to attempt suddenly to recall successfully the teachings of their parents when those children come home for a holiday or birthday visit to "Dad and Mom's" house.[45] "Retain" means to "make it your own" as well as to "receive." In the life of Solomon's son, Rehoboam experienced the negative results of indifference to parental instruction (Rehoboam lost his kingdom, in large part because the people in Rehoboam's kingdom responded to his instructions as Rehoboam responded to his father's instructions—they refused to listen and obey).[46] Picture Solomon's son Rehoboam. When dad or mom was talking,—as children do today—did he roll his eyes, fidget nervously, "stop his ears" to instruction, harden his heart, or stare out the window until dad or mom gave up or finished their "parental" address? Children need to listen with their hearts. "Keep" means to "guard" as would a sentinel who makes secure a priceless possession. In Proverbs 4:5, Solomon issued two commands that every child should establish as lifelong goals: (1) get wisdom! (2) get understanding! Of the two, wisdom is the principal thing because wisdom is "the God-given ability to make God-informed and God-centered decisions in life" (see Proverbs 1:2; 4:7).[47] In Proverbs 4:1–9, in examining the terms, as used in the original Hebrew text, what leaps out from the page?

1. Parents have a responsibility to instruct their children in matters pertaining to biblical wisdom and godly understanding.
2. Children have a responsibility to both receive parental instruction when they are children and retain that instruction—in the form of practical wisdom and daily understanding—for the rest of their lives.

It is never enough for a child to give "lip service" to what he/she has been taught. Parental instruction is meant to be lived and to be seen as a foundation for living. Live God's truth!

Proverbs 4:10–13, 20–23. A child's obedience adds to both the quality and quantity of the child's life.

Hear, my son, and receive my sayings, and the years of your life will be many. I have taught you in the way of wisdom; I have led you in right paths (Proverbs 4:11 identifies what Solomon did for his son, in the past). When you walk, your steps will not be hindered, and when you run, you will not stumble (Proverbs 4:12 speaks of what Solomon's teachings do for his son, in the present). Take firm hold of instruction, do not let go; keep her, for she *is* your life (Proverbs 4:13 speaks of what Solomon's words will do for his son in the future—if the son obeys. Solomon's biblically consistent words of instruction will be the constant guardian of his son's "life"). My son, give attention to my words; incline your ear to my sayings (in order to hear better, "lean one ear in" and "spread it out" like a picnic blanket to be filled with the milk and meat of a father's teachings from God's Word). Do not let them depart from your eyes (since most people are visual, keep them where you can see them—as with the phylactery pouches of Proverbs 3:3); keep them in the midst of your heart (keep them before your eyes—on the outside, and let them "take up residence in your heart"—on the "inside"—by guarding them, in your heart, as would an armed sentinel who keeps priceless possessions secure); For they *are* life to those who find them, and health to all their flesh. Keep your heart with all diligence, for out of it *spring* the issues of life. (Proverbs 4:10–13, 20–23)

The bare-bones statement given by Paul where he instructed children to "'honor (place a high value on) your father and mother,' which is the first commandment with promise: 'that it may be well with you and you may live long on the earth.'" (Ephesians 6:2–3, which is "fleshed out" in Proverbs 4:12–23). If a child wants to live long, prosper, and experience a healthy life, he/she would do well to both learn and live the principles parents teach from scripture. When children obey their parents, they are promised more than (1) an increased quality of existence and (2) a lengthened quantity of years. In addition, an obedient child's "steps will not be hindered" ("impeded, restricted, or filled with obstacles too difficult to overcome") so that, when his/her daily pace increases and life starts to take off, the child will not fall or stumble on the pathway to success (unlike the wicked of Proverbs 4:14–19 who, concerning the ups and downs of life, never seem to figure it out because they walk in darkness instead of the light of God's revealed Word). If, in Proverbs 4:23, the child wants a "spring" in his/her step, that child needs to obey his/her parents in the Lord. That is a principle that lasts a lifetime.[48]

Proverbs 5:1–8, 20. Be constantly vigilant concerning the "crowd" your child keeps and warn your child to flee immorality because immorality is sin.

> My son, pay attention to my wisdom; lend your ear to my understanding, That you may preserve discretion, and your lips may keep knowledge … Therefore hear me now my children and do not depart from the words of my mouth. For why should you, my son, be enraptured by an immoral woman and be embraced in the arms of a seductress? (Proverbs 5:1–8, 20)

Parents have the right to "have a say" in the friends their children select. In warning his son to stay away from immoral people, from experience, Solomon cut to the chase and began chapter 5's teachings by pinpointing a woman's prime source of temptation—the "kiss of her lips" (see Proverbs 5:3–6).[49] Sexual relationships outside of marriage impact negatively the lives of a parent's children. In warning his son about these relationships, Solomon said, in essence, incline your ear to this: "Read *my* lips!" Practice discretion (Proverbs 5:2). Be careful of the crowd you keep (Proverbs 5:7–8). Count the cost of the consequence (Proverbs 5:9–14). Refuse to allow your obedience to be influenced by your emotions (Proverbs 5:20). When you get married, be content with the wife of your youth (Proverbs 5:15–20). When you fail, open your heart to God and allow God to convict you of your sin (Proverbs 5:21–23) "for the ways of a man are [always] before the Lord" (Proverbs 5:21). As one parent said when sending his/her son/daughter out on a date, "We trust you. God sees you. Have a good time." God is watching. To life, apply biblical wisdom (see also Proverbs 6:23–29).

Proverbs 6:1–5, 20–23. Manage your money wisely.

> My son, if you become surety for your friend (if you pledge your money as a cosigner), *if* you have shaken hands in pledge for a stranger, You are snared by the words of your mouth; you are taken by the words of your mouth. So do this, my son, and deliver yourself; for you have come into the hand of your friend: Go and humble yourself; plead with your friend. Give no sleep to your eyes, nor slumber to your eyelids. Deliver yourself like a gazelle from the hand *of the hunter,* and like a bird from the hand of the fowler. My son, keep your father's command, and do not forsake the law of your mother. Bind them continually upon your heart; tie them around your neck. When you roam, they will lead you; when you sleep, they will keep you; and *when* you awake, they will speak with you. For the commandment *is* a lamp, and the law a light. (Proverbs 6:1–5, 20–23)

Being the son of the richest man in the world has both its advantages and disadvantages. For Solomon's son, Rehoboam, he enjoyed the "perks" of palatial living. But because he had access to money he did not earn, Rehoboam became a target of those who wanted money they did not earn. Even when he did not "give his father's money away," it is possible that he cosigned for loans for friends or others who could not repay their debts. If this is true, picture Solomon having a "sit down—heart-to-heart and face-to-face" talk with his son where Solomon addressed Rehoboam sternly and said, "Never cosign for a loan!" Snared by the words of your mouth, you make a promise—to a creditor—to pay another person's debt. If that other person lacks integrity, you will never cosign for another loan again. Instead of loaning money, give it as a gift and trust the person who received the money to demonstrate integrity and restore the money that is/was given. Refuse to squander what God has given. Remove emotions or any "relationship factor" from any real or potential loan agreement.[50] Make realistic arrangements. If you make a mistake when managing God's money, humble yourself, admit your mistake, and seek an equitable financial reconciliation (see Proverbs 6:3–5). In doing so, the child (guards) his parents' instructions (Proverbs 6:20) and "keeps the light on" when confronted by those who desire to take advantage of the financially inexperienced or the gullible (Proverbs 6:23). Because it is the Lord's money in your hands, be a good steward (money manager) of God's gifts (1 Corinthians 4:1–2).

Proverbs 7:1–3, 24–27. Just because a parent made mistakes when he/she was young does not mean that the child must make the same mistakes when he/she is young.

> My son, keep my words, and treasure [up] my commands within you. Keep my commands and live, and my law as the apple of your eye. Bind them on your fingers; write them on the tablet of your heart (make them yours). Say to wisdom, "You *are* my sister," and call understanding *your* nearest kin (closest kin), that they may keep you from the immoral woman, from the seductress *who* flatters with her words. Now therefore, listen to me, *my* children; Pay attention to the words of my mouth: Do not let your heart turn aside to her ways [and] do not stray into her paths; For she has cast down many wounded, and all who were slain by her were strong *men.* Her house *is* the way to hell, descending to the chambers of death. (Proverbs 7:1–3, 24–27)

Just because immoral relationships dominate(d) the life of a parent (in this case Solomon), does not mean that immoral relationships should dominate the life of the child when that child becomes of age or grows.[51] By the time Solomon wrote Proverbs 7, the prevailing themes of sexual immorality, unfaithfulness in marriage, and adulterous affairs were front and center in his mind. Possibly, although he did not have an internet to surf—while standing on the palace rooftop—Rehoboam may have looked down, saw a "woman of the streets" standing at the corner, and, lusting after her, was tempted to disobey his dad's directions and seek her just as David sought Bathsheba (see 2 Samuel 11) and/or as his father, Solomon, sought his concubines.[52] Establish God's truths as the pupil of your eye (Proverbs 7:2). Instead of turning your eyes toward sin, turn your eyes from sin. Refuse to allow even a speck of sin's dust to enter your line of sight (value faithfulness to God's Word as much as you value your eye(s), and you will be kept from sin). Form a relationship with the woman God approves—wisdom (see Proverbs 7:4). When you do, your "sister" wisdom will keep you from sin.[53]

Proverbs 8:1–4, 32. Teach your children to keep their spiritual commitments current and to refuse to compromise with sin.

> Does not wisdom cry out, and understanding lift up her voice? She takes her stand on the top of the high hill, beside the way, where the paths meet. She cries out by the gates, at the entry of the city, at the entrance of the doors: "To you, O men, I call, and my voice *is* to the sons of men. O you simple ones, understand prudence, and you fools, be of an understanding heart. Listen, for I will speak of excellent things, and from the opening of my lips *will come* right things; For wisdom *is* better than rubies, and all the things one may desire cannot be compared with her. Now therefore, listen to me, *my* children, for blessed *are those who* keep my ways. (Proverbs 8:1–4, 32)[54]

Just as the immoral women of Proverbs 5 and Proverbs 7 walked the streets, the twin sisters of "wisdom" and "understanding" walked the same streets. Just as the immoral women of Proverbs 5 and Proverbs 7 "called out *to* men," the sibling sisters of "wisdom"[55] and "understanding"[56] (applied wisdom) went public and "called out men" when they saw those men tempted to compromise their commitment to purity by submitting to temptation, through sin. As if standing on a high hill, God's wisdom is never hard to find. It is as close as a Bible or a godly counselor. As one sister "wisdom" speaks clearly into one ear and, as the other sister "understanding" speaks into the other ear, there is no confusion as to what the "sisters" say: "Keep your spiritual commitments current. Refuse the compromise of sin." If only Samson, David, and Solomon had listened to their "sisters," history would have told a different story about their lives. Since wisdom is "older than dirt" (see Proverbs 8:24) and is older than everything else that God created (see Proverbs 8:22–31), listen to the "spiritual sisters" that God created to help you ("wisdom" and "understanding"). Heed wisdom and understanding's voice(s). Walk in their way.

Proverbs 10:1, 5. Every child's work ethic is a self-portrait of his/her soul.

> The proverbs of Solomon: A wise son makes a glad father, but a foolish son *is* the grief of his mother. He who gathers in summer *is* a wise son; he who sleeps in harvest *is* a son who causes shame. (Proverbs 10:1, 5)

Is it foolishness to be lazy? Knowing that laziness is a sin and that every child's work is a self-portrait of the child's soul, perhaps Rehoboam was the son who slept in harvest, avoided work, and caused his family shame. If so, from Proverbs, here are some characteristics of a sluggard. How many of these characteristics are found in your child(ren)?[57]

1. Proverbs 6:7. Sluggards need others to guide them and rarely plan ahead.
2. Proverbs 6:9. Sluggards love to sleep and have trouble "getting started."
3. Proverbs 10:5. Sluggards waste opportunities.
4. Proverbs 10:26. Sluggards are unreliable, avoid tasks, are a distraction, and refuse to help.
5. Proverbs 12:24–27. Sluggards quit before their work is done and are chronic dependants.
6. Proverbs 13:4. Sluggards want things but refuse to work for them.
7. Proverbs 18:9. Sluggards are costly to business, are expensive to raise, and waste resources.
8. Proverbs 19:15. Sluggards live in poverty. They rarely have enough.
9. Proverbs 19:24. Sluggards put forth little to no effort to meet their basic needs.
10. Proverbs 21:25–26. Sluggards are constantly restless and lack contentment.
11. Proverbs 20:4. Sluggards think of themselves more highly than they ought.
12. Proverbs 22:13. Sluggards make excuses for their lack of involvement.[58]
13. Proverbs 24:10. Sluggards cannot be counted on when things get tough.
14. Proverbs 24:30. Sluggards rarely take care of what they have—often, it is "one and done."
15. Proverbs 26:13–16. Sluggards "know-it-all" and are (often) defensive.

In a parable told by Jesus (Matthew 21:28–32),[59] a vineyard keeper had two sons. One worked. The other did not. Although not named in scripture, one son's name was "Will." The other son's name was, "Won't." "If you called your child by his/her "work ethic," would his/her name be "Will" or "Won't?" Laziness is never blessed by God. Instill in your children a biblical work ethic. Begin the process when they are young, and they will not regret it when they are older.

Proverbs 13:1, 14. Children must do more than humor their parents. Children must honor them.

> A wise son *accepts his* father's discipline, but a scoffer does not listen to rebuke.
> The teaching of the wise is a fountain of life, to turn aside from the snares of death.
> Proverbs 13:1, 14)

As mentioned earlier (in Proverbs 1), the "scoffer" laughs at wisdom, toys with wickedness, and rejects instruction (see Proverbs 1:22, 3:34, 9:7–8, 13:1, 14:6; 15:12, 19:29, 21:24, 22:10, and 24:9). Perhaps, because Solomon's own son listened so little and ignored his father's advice so often, one of Solomon's main themes in Proverbs was: "wise children listen, heed, and obey." Picture Solomon's son, Rehoboam. While Solomon gave him words *directly from the Lord* (the book of Proverbs and every word in it is *inspired* scripture), Rehoboam daydreamed, scoffed at the words of God repeated by his father, and was indifferent to two fathers' words: the words of his human father Solomon and the words of His heavenly Father God. Bored with both fathers' counsel, how different are spiritually indifferent children today? In a world full of dangers and snares, children who spend their time at the fountain of scripture and who heed godly advice will be spared the heartache of misplaced priorities and unbelief. Children must do more than humor their parents. Children must honor them. Otherwise those children are scoffers.[60]

Proverbs 13:24. In being stronger than his/her child's strongest moments, the parent who loves his/her child disciplines, when needed.

> He who spares his rod hates his son, but he who loves him disciplines him promptly. (Proverbs 13:24)

The term *spare* means to "hold back" or "keep back." In the Hebrew, a "rod" was a stick that was used for spanking. The term *hate* means to "treat like an enemy" or "decrease a person's status." *Love* is to "treat as dear." *Discipline* is more than "correction." It is parents "being on the lookout for opportunities to point their child in the right direction." The term *promptly* should be translated "diligently." It speaks of that daily parental commitment to take immediate positive action when warranted and corrective action when needed—whenever, wherever, and whatever—as required. Because children tend to "wear out" their parents before the children are teens, what would happen if the parents "wore out" their children before the children become teens—to the point that, by the time the children do become teens, they know how they are to behave?[61] In other words, be stronger than the child's strongest moments. Treat every "discipline opportunity" as a "priority intervention" that will help your child's future. *Every* time a child needs corrective discipline, address it. *Every* time your child deserves praise, give it also. As a parent, although many families' disciplinary approach is more consistent with society's, the believer's view of child discipline must be consistent with scripture. Although society says that spanking is outdated, scripture approves it (do *you* "Spock" or "spank?").[62] If spanking is outdated, what else in scripture does society disapprove as outdated—the gospel message? Creation? The trustworthiness of scripture? A belief in God or God Himself? In Proverbs 13:24, a father with possibly hundreds of children clearly stated that the parent who withholds correction "hates" his/her child (treats his/her child as a person of lesser "status/worth"). As implied in Proverbs, if you spare the rod, you will spoil your child. (Why is it that just about everything in America is controlled by a switch except our children?) The parent who loves his/her child disciplines, when needed (see Hebrews 12:6).[63] As a result, instead of allowing your children to get their way, point them in the direction of God's way and walk in that way yourself. Apply the rod of correction to the seat of knowledge (indulgent parents who simply reason with their children do not please God). Properly administered, the rod expresses as much love as a hug or a kiss. God, in anticipating child-discipline, gave children a soft spot in just the right place so they won't get hurt. Are you a "(s)parent" or a "parent?" If you were a school teacher, would you be able to tell which children's parents discipline biblically and which children's parents discipline in a manner consistent with society's ever-changing values (in scripture, examine the child-raising failures made by Eli, in 1 Samuel 2:27–36, with his sons Hophni and Phinehas and contrast those failures with the child-raising successes made by Timothy's grandmother Lois and his mother Eunice, in 2 Timothy 1:6)? Parents who love their children do not spoil them—they correct them. Practice healthy and balanced biblical parenting principles and your children will thank you in the end.[64]

Proverbs 14:26–27. God-honoring homes are a child's #1 place of refuge.

> In the fear of the LORD there is strong confidence, and his children will have refuge.
> The fear of the LORD is a fountain of life, that one may avoid the snares of death.
> (Proverbs 14:26–27)

"Fear" speaks of "respect." It is taking God seriously. "LORD" is the name Jehovah. It is the name used when God wants us to know that He is "the God to Whom we give an account." The term "confidence" speaks of "trust" and "reliable security." The term "refuge" dates back to Rehoboam's grandfather David's days when David sought refuge in caves from an ever-pursuing Saul. It makes reference to "a shelter," similar to a cave, where children can hide from harm. God-honoring homes are a child's #1 place of refuge. In a believer's home, children should be able to experience a "sense of security" stubbornly provided by parents whose #1 goal, as parents, is to keep their children safe. Is your home a "safe place" for your child? As a parent, do you take God so seriously that you continually "update" your efforts to provide for your children a place of shelter and refuge from the storms of life that threaten them? For your children, make your home a place of refuge. Society is dangerous enough.

Proverbs 15:20, 32. When children "get their way" when they are young, they will walk in "their own way" when they are older.

> A wise son makes a father glad, but a foolish son despises his mother. He who disdains instruction despises his own soul, but he who heeds rebuke (the term "heed" means to: "acquire," "buy into," or "allow verbal instruction to be birthed in him/her") gets understanding (the lifelong "inclination" and "disposition" to obey).
> (Proverbs 15:20, 32)

A "wise" son is a son who develops the God-given ability to make God-informed and God-centered decisions in life. In the agricultural environment of ancient times, the acquisition of biblical wisdom included "skill development" (teach your child a skill—how to cook, how to build, how to sew, how to fix a vehicle).[65] Have you ever heard a father "brag on" the discernment or accomplishments of his son? Perhaps it is because that son had a wise heart and skilled hands. In contrast, the "foolish son" (the son "sold out" to his own causes) is the insolent son who, once grown, despises his mom (literally: he treats her as "despicable" or as an "embarrassment"), makes fun of her, and mocks her to others and to her face. According to Solomon, the "all-grown-up yet still immature" foolish son will treat his mother with disrespect because, as a child, he "disdained instruction" (treated his mother's instructional moments as a "waste of time" and neglected them). Hidden in the meaning of this Hebrew word *po-re* ("disdained") is the end result of a child's rejection of his mother's advice.

1. As used in Leviticus 10:6, 13:45, and 21:10 of "cutting/removing" hair and in Numbers 5:18 of hair that is "unbraided," the child will "let loose, run free," and be "unrestrained" in his/ her behavior.[66]

2. As used twice in Exodus 32:25 of God's people being so "out of hand" that Moses had to say, "whoever is on the Lord's side—come to me" (Exodus 32:26), the term "disdained"—when brought to its "grown-up" conclusion—carries with it the end result of "letting loose" or "running wild."

3. As used in Proverbs 1:25, 8:33, 13:18, and 15:32, the term "disdained" speaks of children who have "slipped through their parents' fingers." Why is this? It is because the children's parents allowed those children, without confrontation, to "loathe, reject, ignore, [and] treat with indifference" the instructions given by those parents during their children's growing-up years. As a result, when those children become adults, they tend to walk away from the Lord and their parents—treating the authority of both God and their parents with both rejection and disrespect.

Godly counsel is not to be wasted by children. It is valuable to them as adults—especially when those adult children give birth to their own offspring. Yet, wanting their way as children, they go their own way as adults. When disrespect for parental authority is tolerated in a family's tree, it becomes a cycle that condemns to the third and fourth generations (Numbers 14:18). What parents "let their children get away with when their children are young" has a negative impact on their children's children for four generations! Godly parents need to break that cycle now, and recognize that often "bad children *can be* the result of bad parenting."[67]

As a God-guided parent, do more than talk to your children. "Stay at it" and see the instructional process through until the child's rebellious will is broken and becomes lost in God's will for life. Born a sinner, a child begins life with a selfish will. As a godly parent, bend your child's will toward God, seek to lead your child to Christ at the earliest possible age, and, once the child is saved, allow God's indwelling Holy Spirit to be your Helper, in your child's life, to both enable and empower your child to live a life that pleases Christ.[68]

Two are better than one—especially when the influence of God's Holy Spirit is added to the parents' instructions. With God's Holy Spirit indwelling your "saved" child's life, obedience becomes an "inside" job. Since a parent's truest love is often spelled as a four-letter word: T-I-M-E, refuse to allow your child to waste the godly wisdom that you impart as a parent. Intervene early, and often. Because children who dishonor their parents dishonor God also, be stronger than your children's strongest moments "as often" and "as long" as it takes. When you do, your child will bring you joy, not shame. And, always remember: At the *Bema Seat* of Christ where God rewards for service, He will not reward you for "doing your best" as a parent. Because God rewards for faithfulness and because God will not hand out "participation trophies" for parenting, God will reward you for bringing up His/your children "His way" and for "parenting biblically"—in a manner consistent with scripture—for Him.

Proverbs 17:2. The negative patterns children establish while they are young will come back to haunt them when they become adults.

> A wise servant will rule over a son who causes shame, and will share an inheritance among the brothers. (Proverbs 17:2)

Sometimes parents with a rebellious child will treat someone else's respect-filled child better than they would their own child—even to the point of taking that respect-filled child into their home and treating the child as their own. In Rehoboam's case, Solomon had a servant named Jeroboam who fulfilled the role ("earned the status") of a natural-born son in Solomon's home.[69] As a result, Jeroboam was treated as a son and shared in a "brother's inheritance" in Solomon's home. If Rehoboam was the only son in Solomon's home, he would have received 100 percent of the inheritance. If Jeroboam fulfilled the role of a second son, Jeroboam would have received one-third of Solomon's extensive wealth. One can only imagine the resentment Solomon's natural-born son Rehoboam had against Jeroboam if Jeroboam did receive one-third of Solomon's inheritance. The resentment turned to open outrage when the nation's people decided, upon King Solomon's death, that Jeroboam was more worthy of Solomon's throne than was Solomon's natural-born son, Rehoboam. As a result, the kingdom was divided, and Jeroboam reigned over the ten most northern tribes of Israel while Rehoboam was left to rule over the tribes of Judah and Benjamin (see 1 Kings 11–12). Why did this "split" take place? Read the book of Proverbs. Throughout Proverbs, Solomon addressed and described Rehoboam's glaring shortcomings as a son who did not listen, did not obey, and did not work effectively in the home. Rehoboam's lack of integrity and laziness alone were reasons enough to take away his kingdom. The negative patterns children establish while they are young will come back to haunt them when they become adults. Before becoming an adult—to receive God's best—establish biblical patterns when you are young.

Proverbs 17:6. Allow grandchildren to be the "joy" of grandparents.

> Children's children *are* the crown of old men, and the glory of children *is* their father. (Proverbs 17:6)

What picture is seen hanging on the wall in Proverbs 17:6? It is a nuclear family comprised of a grandfather (perhaps David or the father of Rehoboam's Ammonitess mother); the father, Solomon; and Rehoboam, the son. As grandparents, we know the joy of having a grandchild. It is "glad glory" to drop in, give gifts, play with the grandchildren, babysit, establish bonding relationships, and go home when the day is done. Some grandparents enjoy their grandchildren so much that they wish they had the grandchildren first. In a grandchild's mind, the name grandparent is spelled: L-O-V-E. Rehoboam had at least one grandparent. Although confusion exists as to the exact number, Solomon must have had grandchildren—whom he would have enjoyed. Since grandchildren are the "[garland] crown" of an older man, I wonder which crown Solomon cherished the most: the crown which he wore as he reigned over Israel or the "crown of old men" that he enjoyed as a loving and doting grandparent. Then, in Solomon's family picture, I wonder: Did Solomon cringe every time he saw Rehoboam's face hanging on the wall, knowing that Rehoboam was anything but an ideal son? We may learn that answer one day, in the future, in heaven.

Proverbs 17:21, 25, 28. Parents need to do everything they can to raise their children in such a way that the children do not "spoil" but instead leave behind a legacy that honors both God and the family's last name.

> He who begets a scoffer *does so* to his sorrow, and the father of a fool has no joy. A foolish son *is* a grief to his father, and bitterness to her who bore him. Even a fool is counted wise when he holds his peace; when he shuts his lips, *he is considered* perceptive. (Proverbs 17:21, 25, 28)

(Wisely it has been said: "keep your mouth shut and be thought a fool—open your mouth and you remove all doubt"). Because Solomon and Rehoboam's Ammonitess mother did not parent alone, they talked. If there was one topic on which dad and mom agreed, it was this: they had raised a special kind of fool. In modern times, as in the lives of Mr. and Mrs. Solomon, in a parent's mind "the light comes on" that says, "As parents, we failed. When and where did we go wrong?" What is it like to raise a child who always questions and resents/rejects instruction (the scoffer)? What is it like to raise a child who seeks nothing but his/her own way and the pathway of least resistance (the fool)? For the father, it is daily heartache (sorrow and anguish) and a soul-piercing heaviness (grief) that "dries up the bones" (Proverbs 17:22). For the mother, raising a child who disappoints and does not meet even the most basic of expectations is, in Proverbs 17:25, "bitterness" to a mother's soul. The Hebrew word *marah* (in Proverbs 17:25), as in the "bitter waters of Marah" in Exodus 15:22–25,[70] is equated with the "bitter taste of spoiled fruit" (see Deuteronomy 32:32). Born with a mother's high expectations, the child who grows to be a fool leaves such a bad taste in the mother's mouth that she wants to spit it out. Yet who neglected the fruit of the womb to the point that the child became like "spoiled fruit?" Often, spoiled children—like spoiled fruit—leave a bad taste in a parent's mouth because, left unattended or neglected and unnoticed for long periods of time, children—like fruit— become spoiled. "Spare the rod and spoil the child?" Perhaps Solomon had a "spoiled" child on his mind when he authored his passages on discipline. Yet who was guilty of neglect—the parent or the child? Parents appreciate a positive reputation—especially those, like Solomon, who "stood in the gate." Yet, there is something more valuable than a parent's reputation. It is the legacy the parents leave behind in the lives of their son(s) and daughter(s). As parents, we need to do everything we can to raise our children in such a way that they do not "spoil," but instead, in the lives of our children, we need to leave behind a legacy that honors both God and the family's last name. To do so, parents must notice signs of "spoiling" and counteract parental neglect by enacting a "parenting paradigm shift" by investing time in their children.

Proverbs 19:13, 18, 20, 25–27, 29. Parents must agree on a philosophy of discipline: Start early. Be balanced. Correct often.

> A foolish son *is* the ruin of his father, and the contentions of a wife *are* a continual dripping. Chasten your son while there is hope (an optimistic outlook for successful results), and do not set your heart on his destruction. Listen to counsel and receive instruction, that you may be wise in your latter days. Strike a scoffer, and the simple will become wary; rebuke one who has understanding, *and* he will discern knowledge. He who mistreats *his* father *and* chases away *his* mother *is* a son who causes shame and brings reproach. Cease listening to instruction, my son, and you will stray from the words of knowledge. Judgments are prepared for scoffers and beatings for the backs ("backsides") of fools. (Proverbs 19:13, 18, 20, 25–27, 29)

What happens when your child is the child that other parents warn their children about?[71] You experience both anger and frustration. Apparently Solomon and Rehoboam's Ammonitess mother did not agree on a philosophy of discipline. According to Proverbs 19:13, she was "contentious," and her incessant quarreling about discipline methods and other matters was like "a leaking roof" over the couple's bed (perhaps Mr. and Mrs. Solomon should have discussed their "child-discipline" philosophy *before* they got married or, at least, *before* they had a child). In practicing child discipline, notice Solomon's frustration (see Proverbs 19:18). At times, he "set his heart on his son's destruction (*ha-meet*: "death"—at times, he "wanted to kill him")." At what age—how early is too early or how late is too late—should a parent apply the rod of correction to the child's seat of knowledge? Did Solomon wait too long to begin correcting Rehoboam (the term "hope" speaks of "the expectation of an optimistic outcome")? Loving discipline begins at childbirth (it has been said that children are born "spoiled" because, from birth, they have a will that wants his/her way). How soon is too soon to "spank" a child? Start early. Be balanced. Never physically harm your child. Was Solomon concerned that his temper would get the best of him and that Solomon would harm Rehoboam, in anger, for his child's repeated disobedience? As with most parents who spank their children, apparently Solomon's answer was yes (see Proverbs 19:18). Did Solomon do more than spank his child—did he render verbal instructions as well? In spite of the daily frustration caused by the child Rehoboam, because every parent—including Solomon—wants his/her offspring to be "successful" as an adult, this answer is also yes (see Proverbs 19:20). From Solomon's own experience, as a parent, did he realize that "not every child will respond the same way to discipline?" Yes. When disciplined, the "scoffer" who laughs at rebuke will harden his/her heart to corporal correction and verbal instruction. Yet, other children with "softer" hearts are receptive to correction and instruction (see Proverbs 19:25). Concerning children who resent or reject instruction, what does the Bible say? By their hard-hearted response to discipline, according to Proverbs 19:26, those children "mistreat" their father and "chase away" their mother (they "respond violently" to their father and they make the act or process of child discipline so unpleasant for the mother that she "flees" or "runs away" from the scene of discipline due to the child's negative, "hard-hearted," or resent-filled response). How many parents who have raised "unresponsive" children can picture this scene: the father disciplines the child; the child responds in violent verbal or physical anger; and the mother is so distraught by "what just happened" that she turns and runs away?[72] Then Solomon issued two warnings:

1. If the child refuses to listen to his/her parents, the child will "stray away" or "be misled" by other voices (there are thousands of voices clamoring for the child's attention every day (see Proverbs 19:27).
2. If the child insists on resisting a parent's discipline, that child will receive more discipline ("beatings—plural") until the child learns to obey. "Break the will, but not the child." Imagine the time investment required in the life of King Solomon in disciplining his hard-headed and stone-hearted son, Rehoboam. I wonder: how much time was left over to "rule the kingdom?"[73]

Proverbs 20:7. Teach your children to live a life of integrity that is "character driven, not emotion led."

> The righteous *man* walks in his integrity; his children *are* blessed after him. (Proverbs 20:7)

An anonymous poet wrote, "A careful man I want to be — a little fellow follows me. I do not dare to go astray, for fear he'll go the self-same way."[74] The term "righteous" speaks of "one who lives a blameless life." "Walks" speaks of "conduct" or "behavior" (fathers must realize that their children will walk in dad's footsteps—one way or another. Fathers should space their footsteps so that the child's act of "walking in Dad's footsteps" is neither difficult nor overwhelming.). "Integrity" is a public reputation of positive credibility (influence is lost when credibility fails). It is a lifestyle that is so complete that it is honest even when no one but God is looking (image is what people think we are, but integrity is what we really are). It is being a vessel (a jar of clay), separated to God, "without wax" or "without cracks" when held to the light of God's Son (see Philippians 1:10). Integrity is the opposite of hypocrisy. Since children are becoming what they are right now, integrity is what you are in the dark, who you are within, and it is being who you are no matter where you are and no matter who you happen to be with. It is the image of Jesus Christ in the life of the individual believer, being single-minded for God. As a word, *integrity* is taken from the English word *integer*. In math an "integer" is "something that is whole." People of integrity wholly follow the Lord (Joshua 14:8, 9, 14) and are character-driven, not emotion-led. Their life's motto is: "Character, Honesty, Integrity." People who bear the image of Christ, in integrity, continue to practice integrity even when circumstances change. Since the "righteous" (just man who lives a life of innocence) "walks" (conducts himself) with integrity, he has influence (see Proverbs 11:3). Since children do what children see, a father's child becomes a lengthened shadow of his dad. God never said a person must be perfect. But people must have integrity (in minor matters as well as in the major areas of life). That means a father must keep his word, be honest in all dealings (both personal and business), and practice moral purity (both in mind and in body). If the father wants his son to walk in a manner pleasing to God, the father must walk that way himself. Be dependable. Be whole. Be a person of integrity.[75]

Proverbs 20:20–21. A child who is swift to verbally disrespect his/her parent(s) reveals the condition of his/her heart.

> Whoever curses his father or his mother, his lamp will be put out in deep darkness.
> An inheritance gained hastily at the beginning will not be blessed at the end.
> (Proverbs 20:20–21)

When was the last time your child "back-talked" his/her parent(s)? Often rebellious children will swiftly respond in verbal anger or spoken resentment at any corrective instruction. This is exactly what Solomon portrayed in Proverbs 20:20. It is his child "cursing" his father or his mother with "swift speech that slights the character and questions the authority of his/her father or his/her mother." Disrespect for any parent violates God's fifth commandment, "Honor ("place a high value on") your father and your mother, that your days may be long upon the land which the Lord your God is giving you" (see Exodus 20:12). Children who are swift to talk back may get away with it at home, but God is listening. He disapproves of children who disobey, deceive, or disrespect their parents. But God judges those who defame/dishonor their parents. Parents stand in the place of God in the home. Once the children get married, how children treated their parents is (often) how marriage partners will treat their mates. A child who is "swift to verbally disrespect" his/her parent(s) merely reveals the condition of his/her heart and demonstrates a lack of respect for the God who gave the child his/her parent(s). As Solomon wrote, there are at least two consequences for the child (see Proverbs 20:20b).

1. The child's "lamp" will be put out in darkness (like the wick on a lamp, the potential for that child will flicker and then be "destined for obscurity"—the lamp will remain, but, unless "relit" or "reenergized," the "life's vitality" of the child will greatly diminish or "grow dark" in a manner similar to the pupil of an eye not being able to see/comprehend once the eyelid is closed over the pupil).[76]

2. Because fast money ruins immature people and, because people who worship wealth often "lose" it in the end—like the prodigal son who received his inheritance yet burned through it and used it up swiftly, the child who does not listen to the godly counsel of his/her parent(s) may "lose" his/her inheritance through the parents rewriting their will or through the child wasting his/her good inheritance.[77]

Proverbs 20:27, 29–30. When a child makes God the joy of His life, God rewards the child's faithfulness to Him.

> The spirit ("life's breath") of a man *is* the lamp of the LORD (JEHOVAH), searching ("examining and tracking down") all the inner depths ("dark room") of his heart (literally: "the rooms of his belly" or "the seat of a person's desires"). The glory of young men *is* their strength, and the splendor of old men *is* their gray head. Blows that hurt cleanse away evil, as *do* stripes the inner depths of the heart (literally: "the rooms of the belly"). (Proverbs 20:27, 29–30)

As mentioned earlier, a lamp without an available wick gives no light. In the context of "the wicks of life," as a king, Solomon "balanced out" his cabinet of counselors by surrounding himself with both physically strong young people and "wise old heads" (Proverbs 20:29). Hopefully both "age groups" that surrounded Solomon learned to curb their appetites for the things and pleasures of this world. In speaking of the "inner depths of the heart" (literally: "the rooms of his belly" or "the seat of a person's desires"), Solomon made a veiled reference to a man's stomach, which represents a part of the body where something cherished resides—the man's latest meal: food.[78] Why is it said that, "the way to a man's heart is through his stomach?" Perhaps it is because, in an agricultural society as was the society of Solomon's Israel, the most tangible representation of a man's "spoils of his success" went to his stomach. True prosperity comes from the Lord (Joshua 1:6–8). What needs to be digested in the innermost parts of a man is God's Word through prayer and fasting (see Jeremiah 15:16).[79] When a child makes God the joy of His life, God gives more than food. God rewards the child's faithfulness to Him. As a parent, establish and fulfill this goal: help your child establish and develop a close personal relationship with God.

Proverbs 22:1, 6. Because a child "bent" toward Christ will live his/her values when he/she is old, parents have a God-given responsibility to influence that child for the Lord.

> A *good* name is to be chosen rather than great riches, loving favor rather than silver and gold. Train up a child in the way he should go, and when he is old (literally: "old enough to grow a beard") he will not depart from it." (Proverbs 22:1, 6)

As Solomon addressed his son, he wanted Rehoboam to learn some lessons for living, including the following:

1. Because—once compromised—it is difficult to regain, value integrity. In that context, a "name" is a summary statement of everything a person is. What "drives" your child? By what "name" would your child be summarized? Would that name be the name of Jesus or would it be the name on the label of his/her clothes (does he/she more highly regard price tags or values)?[80]
2. Children need to appreciate their upbringing and apply the lessons they learned from dad and mom to life. Since Proverbs 22:6 is considered a "classic" passage on child-raising, what instructions did Solomon give for parents to follow? Let us look at some words.

In Proverbs 22:6, what does it mean to "train?" The term *train* (the Hebrew term *hahnok*) is found five times in the Old Testament. It is used of initiating the use of a building (Deuteronomy 20:5), of dedicating a temple (2 Chronicles 7:5), of making an inner court holy (1 Kings 8:63), and of completing military instruction as a squire (Genesis 14:24). Since saved children are "sanctuary saints," when was the time that you, as a parent, saw your child as a building or a temple whose "inner court" needs to reflect the holiness of God (see Deuteronomy 20:5, 2 Chronicles 7:5, 1 Kings 8:63, 1 Corinthians 6:19–20)?[81] Since the term *train* is used also in the context of a soldier being prepared for battle, in what ways must parents prepare their children to fight the "good fight of faith" as adults (see Genesis 14:24, Ephesians 6:10–18)? Then, in the context of child-raising (in Proverbs 22:6), the term *train* was used of a mother stimulating a baby's desire to eat by using date jam gently rubbed on the gums of a newborn baby to enhance the appetite and introduce the "sucking process" of the child for the mother's milk. Applied spiritually, the training process, provided by parents, should "develop a thirst" for the only way a child should "walk" or go: in "the way" of the Lord.

As mentioned in Proverbs 22:6, what is a child? The term *child* (the Hebrew term *na-arr*) describes any offspring living under the parents' roof. It is an unborn baby (see Judges 13:5–12), a newborn infant (see 1 Samuel 4:21), an infant still unweaned (see 1 Samuel 1:22), Baby Moses at three months old (see Exodus 2:6), Ishmael in his preteen years (see Genesis 21:16), Joseph at age seventeen (see Genesis 37:2), a young man still at home but ready for marriage (Genesis 34:9), and a thirty-year-old still at home (Genesis 41:12, 46). "My house, my rules!" As long as your offspring are under your roof, God expects them to respect your authority. Until the child "leaves the nest," parents have a God-given responsibility to influence that child for the Lord.

In Proverbs 22:6, what is "the way?" In general, a "way" (the Hebrew term *derek*) is a characteristic, manner of living, the child's "journey," or "that which dominates" a person's life. It is a way of life (Proverbs 6:23), of understanding (Proverbs 9:6), and of righteousness/right living (Proverbs 2:20). Elsewhere in Proverbs, knowing that each example mentioned has its own distinctive "way," the term *way* is used of the "way of an eagle" as it soars, the "way of a serpent" as it slithers on a rock, the "way of a ship" as it plies the waves, and the "way of a man" romancing a woman (see Proverbs 30:18–19). Many equate "the way" with "the bent" in a baby, which is the child's affinity toward certain interests in life (athletics, music, creativity, academics, or things that are practical, technical, mechanical, or complex). It is that unique and individualized direction the specific child "should go." As the twig is bent so grows the tree. What a child learns he never forgets. Children left to themselves will be bent in the direction of the influence they receive from society (movies, games, peers, or social media). But a child "bent" toward Christ will live his/her values when he/she is old. In addition, the term *way* is used of the way of an archer as he handles his bow (see Proverbs 7:12). With that in mind, should your children be "shot?" What do I mean by that? How many of you have ever shot an arrow? If the string is too tight, the bow breaks (so will the children). If it is too loose, the arrow misses the target and falls short. But if the string is balanced with the bow *and* the arrow is pointed toward the bull's-eye, the arrow hits its mark. So will your children. Then, concerning a child's "bent,'" a parent must ask: How can a parent or child discover the child's "bent" or "the direction the child should go?" A child's bent is discovered when he/she starts to distinguish himself/herself through actions (see Proverbs 20:11–12). Listen, observe, and discover your child's bent. Then "bend" that child toward God. How is that "bending" accomplished? It is accomplished through observation, communication, education, application, intervention, time, prayer, and consistency of love. If we want our children to walk in God's way, we must walk that way ourselves. That is like the little boy who was jumping in the snow. The mother called out, "What are you doing?" The boy replied, "I'm walking in Daddy's footsteps."[82] More is caught than taught in the home. Discover the child's interest(s). Since God can use any interest your child has for His glory and for the child's good, include the child's interest in "bending" that child toward God.[83]

In Proverbs 22:6, how old is "old?" The Hebrew term for old (*yaz-kin*) speaks of the age a son begins to grow a beard (a male does not start growing a beard at age twenty-five or ninety, but around age fourteen). Many parents raise prodigals and expect their children to return to God when they are older adults. We pray that prodigals will return to the biblical values of their home (praise the Lord—many have!). However Solomon taught in Proverbs 22:6 that a receptive child who is properly taught biblical values by his father and mother will practice those values when he/she is a teen (at the age when a male child first starts to grow a beard). In other words, teenagers are not required to rebel. According to both Solomon and Paul, teenagers can be an "example to the believers in word, in conduct, in love, in spirit, in faith, [and] in purity" (see 2 Timothy 4:12–13). Since what your child is when he/she is age two to four is (often) what that child becomes when he/she is age fourteen to sixteen, invest time with your child while your child is young and that child will "not depart from" ("choose to abolish," "wander away from" or "swerve" and "turn aside from") God's teachings later in his/her life—even as a teen. Since our children are "on loan" from God for eighteen or more years, parents must realize: we have them only for a moment. As a result, parents must take advantage of the time they have and focus children's minds, hearts, wills, and conscience on the world to come as we—as parents—invest our lives in them. From a child's perspective, Rehoboam had his opportunity to listen and heed his parent's advice. He refused and lost his kingdom. Pray that your children will heed.

Proverbs 22.28, 23:10–11. For your children, establish biblical boundaries, enforce them, and keep them in place.

> Do not remove the ancient landmark which your fathers have set. Do not remove the ancient landmark (stone boundary pillars that "mark out" a person's property lines), nor enter the fields of the fatherless; For their Redeemer *is* mighty; He will plead their cause (case) against you (God will protect the less advantaged). Apply your heart to instruction, and your ears to words of knowledge. (Proverbs 22:28, 23:10–12)

Landmarks were property markers that established boundaries. In recognizing that the sins of the culture have become the sins of both the church *and* the family, parents (fathers specifically and especially) need to establish biblical boundaries for their children, enforce them, and keep those boundaries in place. Because society is relentless in its attacks on Christians values, what boundaries should parents establish for their children and for their household? Here are a few boundaries fathers must establish: a belief in the deity of Christ (that Jesus Christ is God); an active separation from sin; biblical moral values of purity, based on holiness; adherence to biblical truth; the conviction that biblical absolutes will never be obsolete; a rock-solid belief in biblical creation, which gives believers the basis for our accountability to God; biblical inerrancy (the fact that God's word is true); the security of God's unconditional love; a recognition of God's loving-kindness—that what God promises, He performs (we have a God Who keeps His Word); the knowledge that prayer moves the heart that moves the hand of God; missions and evangelism; the command to disciple; the conviction of the blessed hope of Christ's return; the empowerment and enablement of God's Holy Spirit; the "product/fruit" of God's Spirit valued and practiced (see the list in Galatians 5:22–23)—biblical priorities (love, grace, faith, mercy, respect, obedience, and hope) and the believer's ability to live in the power of Christ's resurrection each and every day.[84] With these and other biblical boundaries enforced and kept in place, children will have an invisible wall of defense that will keep them from looking like easy prey to their society's predators. As a parent, what landmarks of faith and obedience have you established in your home?

Proverbs 23:13–14, 22:15. Be diligent in your discipline—your child's eternity may depend on it.

> Foolishness is bound up in the heart of a child; the rod of correction will drive it far from him. Do not withhold correction from a child: for if you beat him with a rod, he will not die. You shall beat him with a rod and deliver his soul from hell. (Proverbs 23:13–14, 22:15)

Solomon's cure for a child's foolishness (a child seeking his/her own way) is out of favor with child psychologists. Yet healthy and balanced corporal punishment, properly applied in love, works wonders. Do you love your children? Parents who love their children correct them early, often, and biblically (see Proverbs 13:24). Start early. Stay balanced. Be consistent and reasonable. Spank don't Spock (balanced "biblically consistent" discipline is correction, not abuse). Otherwise it is "too soon old and too late wise." In addition, what is the positive consequence of applying biblical discipline? Solomon wrote that parents will "save [the child's soul] from hell." In the Old Testament, Upper Sheol was Paradise for those who, by faith, were obedient to God's requirements and commands (see Luke 23:43). Every child in Israel wanted to spend his/her eternity in Paradise. Similarly, in the Old Testament, the term *hell* is Hades or Lower Sheol (see Psalm 16:10; Luke 16:23). As an abode of the hereafter, it was the place where people went who did not meet God's requirements of law obedience. In Proverbs 23:13–14, it seems that an Old Testament parent's "diligence in performing discipline" had an impact on a child's eternal future. Properly disciplined, the child would learn an obedience that pleased God. Improperly disciplined, the child would learn a disobedience that would not please God. By faith, obedience resulted in Upper Sheol (Paradise). Disobedience resulted in Lower Sheol (hell).[85] Imagine the motivation lines used by Old Testament parents: "Obey or perish!" Children are living clay. The reason parents correct at the beginning of their children's lives is to make sure that their children have a happy ending to their lives. Children who submit to parental authority are more likely to submit to God's authority (submission to any type of authority is lacking in society today). Set limits. Influence habits. Instill truth. Extend love. Expect obedience. Since children need direction, provide it. Ground your children in God's truth. Address every incident. If your child is obedient, praise your child. If your child is disobedient, correct your child. Align your children with the Word and will of God. Your child's eternity may depend on the job you do as a parent (see Proverbs 23:14).

Proverbs 23:22–28. Obedient children cause their parents to be glad.

> Listen to your father who begot you ("conceived" you), and do not despise ("hold in contempt") your mother when she is old ("advanced in years"). Buy the truth, and do not sell *it, also* wisdom and instruction and understanding. The father of the righteous will greatly rejoice, and he who begets a wise *child* will delight in him. Let your father and your mother be glad, and let her who bore you rejoice. My son, give me your heart, and let your eyes observe my ways. For a harlot *is* a deep pit, and a seductress *is* a narrow well. She also lies in wait as *for* a victim, and increases the unfaithful among men. (Proverbs 23:22–28).

In the context of showing deep respect for the now-aged mother who held Solomon's child on her knee and taught his one-to-five-year-old child the first five books of the Bible (The Pentateuch), we ask these questions:

1. Who spoke to Rehoboam in Proverbs 23:24–25? Solomon and the Ammonitess woman (Rehoboam's dad and mom).
2. Who spoke to Rehoboam in Proverbs 23:26–28? God (the Lord knew what Solomon did not know. He knew the weakness of a child's heart).

Since God knew that what Rehoboam saw with his eyes would affect his heart and that what affected Rehoboam's heart would affect his actions also, God demanded of Rehoboam what God demands of us: Give me your heart! When a child loves God more than he/she loves anything else, including himself/herself, God will bless your child's life. That blessing starts with the child's eyes. In Genesis 3:6, Eve saw the forbidden fruit and took it. In Genesis 13:10, Lot lifted up his eyes and saw a land that was the well-watered plain of Sodom. He wanted it and left the altar of God. In Genesis 22:8, 13, Abraham lifted up his eyes and saw that God had provided a sacrificial lamb, and Abraham built an altar. God blessed Abraham's life. What do your eyes see? Is your view horizontal (earth-bound) or vertical (toward heaven)? Do you live for things of the earth or God? Obviously, in a day and age long before children "surfed" the internet, Rehoboam used his eyes to see some women. What did Solomon say about Rehoboam's women? Although the term can be used also of a male (see Exodus 34:16, Numbers 25:1), normally the term "harlot" makes reference to a "female prostitute" who performs "outside-of-marriage" physical acts with a man—for hire (see Deuteronomy 23:19). To his son, Solomon warned that these women were people who were not to be pursued but shunned (see Proverbs 23:27), because both fornication before marriage and adultery after marriage is sin (see 1 Thessalonians 4:1–7, Romans 7:2–3). Yet Rehoboam had an eye for women, which begs this question: "Was this another case of "like father, like son"? Did Solomon have problems also with pursuing women who were not his wife?" With so many wives and concubines, what kind of moral example was Solomon to Rehoboam, his son? In telling his son to "observe my ways," was Solomon teaching his son, by Solomon's bad example, that there are lifelong negative consequences to participating in sins of immorality or by submitting to other categories of sin or temptation? Was it consistent for Solomon to expect to have a "wise" son when Solomon himself, while possessing all the wisdom God could give, could not overcome his own sin nature alone (on his own, without God's help) and acted "unwisely" with women so often that his son, Rehoboam, (possibly) considered "immorality" as acceptable behavior? It is not enough to tell your children how to live. Because more is caught than taught in the home, it is essential that children see godly living modeled in the lives of the parents in the home. Watch your eyes—especially with the internet or other screen choices—because your eyes can affect your heart. Be righteous. Get properly aligned with God.[86]

Proverbs 24:21–22. A child must not trust the influence of those who advise the child to put aside parental authority for an authority outside the home.

> My son, fear the Lord and the king; do not associate (become companions) with those given to change; For their calamity will rise suddenly, and who knows the ruin those two can bring? (Proverbs 24:21–22)

In the context of taking "the long view" on people who demand changes in biblical standards or in government, Solomon admonished His son to respect the two greatest societal authorities in his life: God and Israel's political leader (Solomon the king). In doing so, he told his son to have more respect for stable persons (God and the king) than for restless or rebellious persons—especially those who are given to "revolutionary change" (such as the people in 1 Kings 18:21 who were living out this Hebrew word *senayim* and were given to "societal upheaval"). The reader can almost hear Solomon sternly reminding his son, "Rehoboam, you are living in a household with a father who is a believer. God is your ultimate authority. He sets up and He puts down (see 1 Samuel 2:7–8). Also, you live in the household of your nation's king—a position that you yourself will hold one day. Lead a quiet and peaceable life (see Romans 12:18, 1 Thessalonians 4:18). Acknowledge God as the leader in your home. Teach your people, in God's nation, to respect your leadership as king" (see 1 Timothy 2:1–3). Since Rehoboam would one day be his nation's "top leader," Solomon warned his son that if, publicly, he joined with those who oppose the policies or person of the current king, others "given to revolutionary upheaval" would oppose Rehoboam also when Rehoboam becomes king.[87] Picture Solomon giving to Rehoboam this same advice that every parent should give to his/her son/daughter: "Consider the long view. Think beyond the moment." The required oversight of some children is constant. Solomon had a kingdom to rule. Yet he could not rule his own son—primarily because, as the son of a "mixed spiritual marriage" between a believing Jewish man and an unbelieving Ammonitess woman. Rehoboam chose often the ways of the unbeliever. Ultimately, in fulfillment of Solomon's words in Proverbs 24:22, Rehoboam's lack of discernment—concerning his chosen crowd—came back to haunt him. Rehoboam lost his kingdom to people given to revolutionary change (see 1 Kings 12:6–17 where Rehoboam "rejected the advice which the elders had given him, and consulted the young men who had grown up with him, who stood before him." And, casting off allegiance to God's chosen descendant of David, the people followed the servant Jeroboam, who divided the kingdom and ruled in Rehoboam's place). How many parents, when given the opportunity, could look back on the advice rejected by their children and, seeing the results, say what must have been on Solomon's heart, "See, I told you so and, my son, you did not listen. Now, suffering the consequences of your actions, repent before it is too late." Never trust a person who betrays the trust of godly parents or of God. When they do, your children's "calamity" (stressful times that result in disaster) are sure.

Proverbs 27:11. Every parent with a disobedient child can feel Solomon's pain.

> My son, be wise, and make my heart glad, that I may answer him who reproaches
> me. (Proverbs 27:11)

What parent hasn't been approached by his/her child's school teacher and heard one or both of these statements from that teacher: "Your child was a blessing in class today." That is a statement that causes your heart to rejoice. Or, "We need to talk. Your child made some bad decisions today, was disruptive in class, and misbehaved." That statement makes your heart grieve, which is a word that always involves emotions. In other words, "Rehoboam, it gladdens my heart when you make God-informed and God-centered decisions in life. But when you leave out God in the choices you make, the people who criticize you also criticize me—the parent—and, whether directly or indirectly, they question me about my role as a good parent."[88] Some may say, "Everyone is doing it," yet, if your child is not doing "it," then "everyone" is not doing it. Consistent respect for parental authority and godly discipline is a parent's delight.[89] Children who resist temptation and stand against the negative influences and pressures of the crowd (their misdirected peer group) are like "merry medicine" to a parent's heart (see Proverbs 17:22). Teach your children to "stand in the gap—for God" because, with Christ on board the vessel of his/her life, that child will never stand alone.

Proverbs 27:23–24. Children are like lambs—lead them, feed them, and tend them as a shepherd tends his flock (children need the nurturing of parents).

> Be diligent to know the state of your flocks, and attend to your herds; For riches are
> not forever, nor does a crown endure to all generations. (Proverbs 27:23–24)

Since real wealth is never in houses or lands but in God and your offspring, refuse to neglect the "lambs/children" God gave you. Invest time in shepherding the flock within your home. Lead them. Feed them. Tend them as Grandfather David tended his flocks (see Psalm 23). Then, in a veiled prophesy concerning Rehoboam's future loss of his kingdom, Solomon reminded his son that even "birthrights" do not endure from generation to generation. Be diligent: royalty's right can be removed.

Proverbs 28:7. The stings of a child's unwise actions can leave permanent scars on the hearts of his/her parents.

> Whoever keeps the law *is* a discerning son, but a companion of gluttons shames his father. (Proverbs 28:7)

To "keep the law" is to live out scripture and walk wisely in the direction God commands. "Discernment" is an understanding of circumstances that sees beyond the surface level to the layers underneath (it is thinking like a chess master as it pertains to "what is around the next bend" in life). To be a "companion" means to be "mixed up with." "Gluttons" are people "lacking in moderation and given to excess"—whether in what they eat or in what they desire. "Shame" (the Hebrew word *kalam*) is "humiliation, embarrassment, an insult, a wounded heart or an action that leads to disgrace." In Jeremiah 23:40, it is used of "an everlasting reproach and a perpetual shame, which will not be forgotten." Often the stings of a child's unwise actions leave permanent scars in the life of the parent. Unless laid at the foot of the cross, the scars left behind by a "wild child" rarely heal. Just as parents will answer to God for how they functioned as parents, children will answer to God for how they responded to the authority and advice given by their parents. Each will answer, individually, for themselves. Therefore, to avoid present and future shame, both children and parents should make it their life's pattern to consistently obey God.

Proverbs 28:24. In the life of a child, for every privilege there is an equal responsibility.

> Whoever robs his father or his mother, and says, "*It is* no transgression," the same is companion to a destroyer. Proverbs 28:24

To "rob" means to "plunder." In that regard, a child can "plunder" a parent's emotions just as easily as that child can plunder a parent's possessions. In addition, a child can "use up" or literally "suck out" (the Hebrew term *go-zeel*) a parent's wealth, time, or "life vitality" through constant distractions or demands.[90] What parent has not heard of a child who takes advantage of the goodness and grace of a parent and, viewing the use of a parent's possessions as a right instead of as a privilege, the child treats everything the parent has as his/as hers and "drains the parents dry. "Wealthy beyond imagination," Solomon called this "breach in a trusted relationship" a "transgression" that is *pay-sah*, the Hebrew word for "rebellion." Who hasn't dreaded having a child with this perspective: "But, Dad! But, Mom! Since your house is my house and what is yours is mine, I am entitled to raid your wallet or eat, as a midnight snack, the leftovers that you were saving for tomorrow night's dinner." Children need to learn that, even on this side of the parents' funerals—long before the parents' will is read—parents decide what the child gets (while the parents are still alive). Children need to understand that some of the parents' possessions will not be used today—they will be inherited later. If your child is so entitled as to think that everything belongs to him/her—without restrictions or limits—then you have spoiled your child into thinking that he/she will be entitled to "other people's rights or possessions" for the rest of his/her life. Break the cycle early, and your child will respect the property of others. Otherwise, your child will become "mixed up with" or "a companion to" others just like him/her who think nothing must be earned, that life owes him/her a living—apart from work—and that everything, as a privilege, will be handed to them on a silver platter. That is a child who "destroys" (the Hebrew term *mas-hit*) or "leaves a trap as if snaring a bird." As a parent, be careful not to be caught in the traps your children intentionally or unintentionally set. In the life of a child, for every privilege there is an equal responsibility.

Proverbs 29:1–3. God will remove His blessing on children who, without repentance, harden their hearts toward Him.

> He who is often rebuked, *and* hardens *his* neck, will suddenly be destroyed, and that without remedy. Whoever loves wisdom makes his father rejoice, but a companion of harlots wastes his wealth. (Proverbs 29:1–3)

The term *rebuked* (the Hebrew term *tokeha*) includes an "argument or statement that exposes a person's sin and calls the person to repentance." The term "hardened" speaks of one who is stubborn or stiff-necked like rebellious oxen who refuse to move or like calf-worshiping Israel that quickly turned aside from the Lord's service (Exodus 32:9).[91] The most famous example of a "hardened neck" is Egypt's Pharaoh who stubbornly refused to submit to God's command to "let [God's] people go" (Exodus 13:15). Then, the term "destroyed" makes reference to "something that is broken in pieces like a breach in a wall that leads to a city's destruction, the breaking of a child's will, of a person's heart, or of the breaking of waves on a shoreline." People, who refuse instructions from the Lord, as given by godly parents or others, will be "ruined without remedy." The phrase "without remedy" (the Hebrew term *marpē*) speaks of a "forfeiture of health" or "the removal of the possibility of healing" (see Jeremiah 8:25, Proverbs 4:22). Sometimes, as with Egypt's Pharaoh, the hardening of a person's spiritual arteries is terminal and, without repentance, becomes beyond repair. With that in mind, there is a point in time when a person refuses God's guidance so strongly that God "turns away" and leaves the person to the logical consequences of the person's refusal to submit to God (see Romans

1:18–32). This hardening, without repentance, can happen in the hearts of children. Sometimes, the consequences are physical, as well.

Proverbs 29:15, 17, 21. In understanding that it is never too late to start parenting correctly, be a parent not a "(s)parent."

> The rod and rebuke give wisdom, but a child left to himself brings shame to his mother. Correct your son, and he will give you rest; yes, he will give delight to your soul. He who pampers his servant from childhood will have him as a son in the end. (Proverbs 29:15, 17, 21)

As mentioned previously, (see comments on Proverbs 13:24), a "rod" was a peeled stick used for spanking. "Rebuke" (the Hebrew term *to-ke-hah*) is "a spoken word that includes advice and counsel." Together, measured corporal punishment *and* verbal counsel "give" or "place" wisdom into the heart of a child, with "biblical wisdom" being "the God-given ability to make God-informed and God-centered decisions in life." In contrast, the (s)parent who ignores the child's need for discipline causes his/her child to bring his/her mother "shame" (the Hebrew term *me-bis*) or "humiliation and disgrace." What causes this shame? Shame is caused when the parent's child is "left to himself," which, in the original language, speaks of the child who is allowed "to get his own way" or "be free to pursue his/her own devices" (see Psalm 106:15 where God gave Israel their requests ("what they begged for") but brought leanness ("calamity") into their soul as God troubled His people for rejecting His authority and their accountability to Him). In expressing His perspective on those times when His people refused to heed, obey, and respect the authority of the Lord, God said, "But My people would not heed My voice, and Israel would *have* none of Me. So I gave them over to their own stubborn heart, to walk in their own counsels. Oh, that My people would listen to Me, that Israel would walk in My ways" (Psalm 81:11–13). Then Solomon added words of comfort to parents who biblically discipline their children. In Proverbs 29:17, to "correct" means to "verbally admonish, reprove, and punish" or "warn" (the Hebrew term *yas-seri*). "Rest" is the name "Noah" who, as the captain of God's ark, "made an alliance with His [heavenly] authority" and found "a safe place" where He could "settle down" (see Genesis 6–9, 8:4). Before and during the flood, biblical Noah experienced persecution, trials, tribulation, hard times, and turbulence on the sea. Yet, when his boat "settled down" on Ararat and Noah "brought his family through" (which included his three sons), peaceful times were his. In your chosen method of child-raising, do it biblically: form an alliance with God. Follow His instructions and God will "give" or "place" His "delight" in your soul.[92] In other words, if you discipline your children biblically, you will have a much easier time living with your conscience once your children come of age, become adults, move out of your house, and leave your nest. And, specifically, if you do discipline your children biblically, a father's sons will "be in alignment" with their dad when the children get older (they will be friends). Form an alliance with God. Never parent alone. Network with the Almighty. Understand that it is never too late to start parenting correctly. Be a parent not a (s)parent. Hold your children accountable. Refuse to let "guilt feelings" or "parental shortcomings" hold you back from doing what is right "the next time." Refuse to faint in the "day of adversity" (see Proverbs 24:10). Care enough to confront—especially when it is difficult. Even though your "already reared" children whom you brought up may "rebel" against both you and God (see Isaiah 1:2), wake up every morning renewing your commitment to being a faithful parent for God. Since your children are merely "on loan from God," keep your parental commitments current. Parent for the Lord.

Proverbs 30:1, 11–15. Because God, not society, establishes a parent's guidelines for "all things children," be faithful to God and "stick by the stuff."

> The words of Agur the son of Jakeh, *his* utterance … *There is* a generation *that* curses its father, and does not bless its mother. *There is* a generation *that is* pure in its own eyes, *yet* is not washed from its filthiness. *There is* a generation—oh, how lofty are their eyes! And their eyelids are lifted up. The leech has two daughters—Give *and* Give! (Proverbs 30:1, 11–15)

In bringing his "Parenting by the Book" study guide to its conclusion, a son (Solomon) wrote to others' sons as the words of Proverbs 30 are merely statements written down by Agur whose name means "one who is hired." Perhaps, by this time, Solomon was so "worn out" raising his son Rehoboam that he hired someone else to take dictation and write down what Solomon said. Regardless of whose human words these are, Proverbs 30:1–33 remain the words of God to be respected, applied, and obeyed.[93] What are some of the words that Solomon's amanuensis uttered/said out loud? Beginning in Proverbs 30:11, Solomon, through Agur, stated that an entire generation of children exists who "curse" their parents and who make those parents feel "insignificant" or "worthless." What parent has not looked in the mirror and said, "Parenting seems like a waste of my time and God's effort." Yet that perspective did not come from God. That perspective is the manipulative result of children who are "pure" in their own "eyes ("understanding") and "thumb their noses" at parental authority. Be stronger than your child's strongest moment(s). Refuse to be influenced by the disrespectful responses or attitudes of indifferent-to-discipline children.[94] Stand by the stuff. Continue to parent—even when it is hard. Then Solomon described his generation of offspring as "proud" and "greedy" (see Proverbs 30:13, 15). "Pride *goes* before destruction, and a haughty spirit before a fall" (Proverbs 16:18). Because God does not tolerate pride in heaven or on earth, every generation is but one generation from destruction. Since the family is the foundation on which society is built, refuse to allow your child's generation to become the "terminal" generation. Refuse to spoil your daughters or satisfy your child's every appetite, especially when he/she makes unreasonable demands and says,

"Give to me … Give to me!" (see Proverbs 30:15). Take back society by taking back the family. God, not society, establishes a parent's guidelines for "all things children."

Proverbs 30:17. To prevent society's predators from targeting successfully your children, remain faithful in your responsibility to parent biblically.

> The eye ("center of understanding") *that* mocks ("twinkles as with laughter" or "holds in derision") *his* father, and scorns obedience to *his* mother ("despises, holds as insignificant, holds in contempt" or "brings a sense of alienation"), the ravens of the valley will pick it ("pluck it") out, and the young eagles will eat it. (Proverbs 30:17)

Imagine a parent today saying these words to his/her child: "If you don't obey, a little bird will sit on your nose and peck out your eyes." The modern-day child would laugh at you. However, in Solomon's day, ravens (crows) and eagles did peck out people's eyes when, after a battle, weakened solders lay on the battlefield exhausted. Unable to defend themselves, after the battle, the soldiers would be blinded by fowl predators who laid in wait.[95] So too, in parenting, *after* the battle with your child, when both sides are left exhausted from constant conflict—especially when your children are teens—society's predators lay in wait to increase the spiritual blindness of every child who refuses or rejects biblical parental discipline or who disrespects parental authority. For that reason, it is of utmost importance that parents remain faithful in the discipline of their children.

Proverbs 31:1–3. Since children tend to repeat their unrepentant or unbelieving parents' mistakes, if you want your children to walk in the ways of the Lord,—as a parent—you need to walk in God's ways yourself.

> The words of King Lemuel, the utterance which his mother taught him: What, my son? And what, son of my womb? And what, son of my vows? Do not give your strength to women, nor your ways to that which destroys kings. (Proverbs 31:1–3)

Who was King Lemuel?[96] Some believe that Lemuel was an Ishmaelite, foreign king, or another name for Agur. However most believe that Lemuel was Solomon's pen name, under which he wrote Proverbs 31. If so, the king wrote as a father (in Proverbs 31:1–9) and as a husband (in Proverbs 31:10–31). As a father-husband, Solomon knew that little eyes watched him, followed in his footsteps, and, functioning as both father and husband, Solomon needed to be a role model for his children so that, when his son came of age, that son, Rehoboam, would be a godly father and a loving husband before his children as well.[97] Picture Solomon and his Ammonitess wife approaching their son. Wringing her hands, as do modern-day parents, the Ammonitess mother reminded her disobedient son that she birthed him ("son of my birth pains"), that Solomon and she had dedicated him to God ("son of my vows"), and that a parent's heart was broken because her son had given his heart to another woman, outside the home, who was just as lost and idolatrous as his mom. Children tend to repeat their unrepentant or unbelieving parents' mistakes. If you want your children to walk in the ways of the Lord, as a parent, you need to walk in God's ways yourself. Otherwise, since more is caught than taught, your child will become you. Practice godly morals. Concerning physical relationships, reinforce biblical standards, and teach your children that "true love" waits.[98] Love your child so much that you are willing to sacrifice your pursuits and your wants because of his/her emotional and spiritual needs.[99]

Proverbs 31:10, 28–29. In a child's mind, there is nothing more precious than a godly mother.

> Who can find a virtuous (excellent) wife/[woman: *KJV*]? For her worth *is* far (in distance) above rubies. Her children rise up and call her blessed; her husband *also*, and he praises her: "Many daughters have done well, but you excel (exceed) them all." (Proverbs 31:10, 28–29)

Have you ever been in a public assembly or in a church setting where a child stood up and gave a glowing testimony or report about his/her mom? This is the occasion, in Proverbs 31:28, where the virtuous woman's child stood up publicly and praised his/her mom. When the child did that, the mother's heart must have burst with joy. If, as a child, you want to give your mother a memory that lasts, refuse to wait until Mother's Day. Praise God for her every day, and, often, do it publicly. The term "blessed" (*a-sar*) means "to consider oneself fortunate" or "to be happy" to have her as your mom. That's not all. It does not end there. The husband joins the chorus and "praises" or "boasts about" the mother too. If men get fulfillment from their careers or job, women get satisfaction from commitments made to them and from the security of knowing they are loved. Moms need to hear, "I love you" as often as possible from their children and from the man whom she married. The praise, recorded in Proverbs 31:29, is so special that both the child and the husband acknowledge that, although numerous daughters have done nobly ("virtuously"), his wife and his child's mom "excel" them all (standing at the top of the podium in "the mother's hall of fame," she exceeds them all).[100] With that in mind, in what ways did this mother excel? According to Lemuel (Solomon), the ideal wife and mother excelled in the following ways:

1. She was devoted to her husband (Proverbs 31:10–12). She had a lifetime marital commitment that was modeled before her children. In modern society, would there be fewer divorces experienced by a parent's offspring if the parents of the offspring modeled the same "lifetime marital commitment" as did the Proverbs 31 woman? In Proverbs 31:10, the term "virtuous" speaks of noble character, moral excellence, and of a person of spiritual strength. As a man

who tried one thousand women and didn't find one to match, Solomon said that this virtuous woman was so rare that she was as hard to discover as "rubies," which refers to the rare coral that was taken from the city of Elath on the Gulf of Aqaba in the south of Israel. To get that coral, a person had to sacrifice, suffer, and dive for it. When saying that this Proverbs 31 wife was "of far more value than rubies," Lemuel (Solomon) used the same term translated "cornerstone" (the Hebrew term *peninim*) which made reference to Jesus Christ in Psalm 118:22. Like Christ, a good wife can function as a rock of stability in the home. The term was used also of the only other person in scripture said to be more precious than rubies: wisdom (see Proverbs 3:15, 8:11). As a husband, Lemuel (Solomon) was thankful that his wife was more than just an "attractive" woman. This Proverbs 31 woman was a submissive wife of distinctive discernment who was dedicated to her husband for life. Is this type of woman out there to be discovered today? Absolutely, yes! But, what about people who object or say that it was impossible for this Proverbs 31 woman to be one person—that she had to be a compilation of many women, yet described as one? In scripture, in using the same term as was used in Proverbs 31:10, both men and women were called "virtuous." In the Old Testament, the same term, "virtuous," (the Hebrew term *hay-yil*) was used of the men who were the spiritual leaders of Israel on their journey out of Egypt (see Exodus 18:21). They were men of "virtue" who shared the same qualities as the New Testament's first "deacons" who were chosen to help the apostles (see Acts 6:1–7). They were "men of honest report" (sold out to Christ's cause), "filled with the Holy Spirit" (surrendered, yielded, and plugged into the Holy Spirit's control), and "men of wisdom" (people of discernment who were good at business, managed their lives well, and respected the ways and authority of God). Concerning women, God identified, by name, a "flesh and blood" virtuous woman. Through the kinsman-redeemer Boaz, God said, "Do not fear [Ruth] … for all the people of my town know that you *are* a virtuous woman" (see Ruth 3:11). Just as Boaz found his "virtuous" woman, Solomon was desperate to find his virtuous woman. Yet, among his one thousand wives and concubines, he mentioned one virtuous woman only: the Proverbs 31 woman. It is a sad commentary on any society to know that biblically "virtuous" women are so rare and hard to find. Yet, just as a diver rejoices when he finds that "ruby" or "piece of Aqaba coral," a biblically virtuous woman is always worth waiting for, though difficult to find. In modern times, may her number increase!

2. She gave her husband peace (Proverbs 31:11–12). When Lemuel was away at work and his wife was home alone or she was "out and about" shopping or serving in the community, Lemuel trusted her love to be committed/sure (Proverbs 31:11) and their mutual love to be secure (Proverbs 31:12). With a thousand wives and concubines, Solomon never knew fully that he could trust any member of his harem to be loyal or pure. Desperately, Solomon wanted a bond between himself and a wife who had integrity. Yet, never having found that

wife previously, Solomon would write, "[There is one thing] … which my soul still seeks, but I cannot find: One man among a thousand I have found, but a woman among all these I have not found" (Ecclesiastes 7:28). How sad! Instead, being "more bitter than death," Solomon found "the woman whose heart is snares and nets, whose hands are fetters" ("chains that bind" as if the man is a prisoner in his own house; see Ecclesiastes 7:26). No matter how many non-Proverbs 31 women he married, Solomon was a miserable man, always looking for "Mrs. Right." If only Solomon had realized that Mrs. Right's beauty was more than skin deep, he would have found her if only he had fallen in love with a heart in love with God.[101] Headship is not hardship. As a wife, give your husband peace, and he will be a blessing to your life ("[it is] better to dwell in a corner of a housetop, than in a house shared with a contentious woman" (see Proverbs 21:9).

3. She delighted in her work. "She seeks wool and flax, and willingly works with her hands. She is like the merchant ships; she brings her food from afar. She also rises while it is yet night, and provides food for her household, and a portion for her maidservants" (Proverbs 31:13–15). A virtuous woman cares for those in her home. Although some may scoff at the statement that "a man may work 'til setting sun, but a woman's work is never done," the virtuous woman often does "beat her husband up" in the morning (she arises from bed before he does). In Proverbs 31:13–15, what did this woman do? She went shopping for her family. She used her hands skillfully. In an age before social media, she was productive, not lazy, and "willingly worked" with her hands—without distraction (Proverbs 31:13). Where did this woman go? This virtuous woman was focused. She did not "waste away" her days gossiping with neighbors or friends. She was bargain hunting and knew the value of a shekel. If she lived today, she would "clip coupons" or seek out discounts (Proverbs 31:14). When did this woman begin her day? Not known to oversleep, this woman got the most out of her life by being the first in her family to say, "Good morning" to God (she must have had devotions). She arose, while it was night, and gave assignments to her maidens, who might have made her a specialist in preparation and administration (she had positive management skills). In a timely manner, she got things done. What is the quietest time in your household? As with this Proverbs 31 household, it is probably late at night—after the kids go to bed—or early in the morning before the children get up. Other than wrapping up the day at night or getting ready for the day in the morning, what else do you think this woman was doing during those "quiet times?" At night, she was thanking God for the day. In the morning, she was spending some time with God preparing her soul for the day. Any woman who has a close relationship with God is a woman worth pursuing.[102]

4. She had a disciplined routine. "She considers a field and buys it; from her profits she plants a vineyard. She girds herself with strength, and strengthens her arms. She perceives that her merchandise *is* good, and her lamp does not go out by night. She stretches out her hands

to the distaff, and her hand holds the spindle. She extends her hand to the poor, yes, she reaches out her hands to the needy" (Proverbs 31:16–20). Here was woman with a plan. Living in an age prior to shrink wrap, far-in-the-distance expiration dates, freeze-dried food, refrigerators, freezers, or any other time-saving, food-preserving modern inventions, she managed her time by planning her work and working her plan. What was this woman's purchasing pattern (Proverbs 31:16)? Other than knowing a good buy when she saw it, she made investments that increased in value. When she purchased land, she did it with the goal of planting a vineyard to bring in extra cash for the home. She was a working woman who labored with one goal in mind: to decrease her husband's burden in providing for their home. What was the physical condition of this woman (Proverbs 31:17)? She was not someone who lacked exercise or who sat around the tent all day eating Jewish treats. Far from lazy, she "worked out" and did not "let herself go" after she was married. Emotionally, she was fit, as well. What was the reputation of this Proverbs 31 woman (Proverbs 31:18–19)? Her merchandise was good. She did not fall prey to passing fads or gimmicks. She was rarely bored. Because she had developed some job skills, she ran a business from her home. She discovered something to do. What was her perspective on people outside her home (Proverbs 31:20)? She was not greedy. She helped the needy. With the overflow from her home, this woman shared. Did she help others alone? Certainly, as an example, she included her children in reaching beyond themselves to meet the needs of people less fortunate than they. Selfless compassion is a virtue that is never out-of-date. Order your priorities. Appreciate your beauty as a woman of excellence. Have hands that work while having a heart for God. As God provides, be a domestic engineer. Make a difference through your work.

5. She dressed with care. "She is not afraid of snow for her household, for all her household *is* clothed with scarlet. She makes tapestry for herself; her clothing *is* fine linen and purple. Her husband is known in the gates, when he sits among the elders of the land. She makes linen garments and sells *them,* and supplies sashes for the merchants. Strength and honor *are* her clothing; she shall rejoice in time to come" (Proverbs 31:21–25). Here is a woman who smiles at the future, has a sense of humor, and is not too self-absorbed to laugh. Her family is properly clothed. What do we know about this biblically virtuous wife?

1. She is ready for the winter (Proverbs 31:21). Although the average yearly snowfall in Jerusalem was five inches, it did get cold. This woman watched the "weather reports." She made sure that her children had "boots" and a second layer of clothing. When her shepherd husband got home from the fields, she had the "hot chocolate" waiting on her tenth century BC stove. She planned ahead, took precautions, and thought through details. Concerning her children's clothes, they were "scarlet" which was a dye obtained from the crushing of worms. That took work. Concerning this scarlet dye, it was mentioned by a prophet when he wrote, "Come now, and let us reason together, says

the Lord, though your sins are like scarlet (the color of the dye from the crushed worms used to produce the scarlet), they shall be as white as snow" (Isaiah 1:18). In heaven, believers get a change of garments too.

2.   She is respected in the community (Proverbs 31:22–25). When Lemuel (Solomon) was on his palace balcony looking out over the streets of Jerusalem, he spotted his ideal woman. What did he say about her?

   a.   She knew how to dress. Coverings of tapestry and garments of linen/silk were not cheap. They honored her husband. A woman should dress to honor her husband only and be a reflection of grace.

   b.   b. She encouraged her husband's strengths. While he sat at the gate among the community leaders where important decisions were made, she did nothing to harm him and everything to enhance his positive reputation. When people ask you, "You are married to whom?" you need to realize that you are known by his name.

   c.   c. She is a gifted worker and emotionally stable. Her line of clothing sells. Her best garment is her solid and stable character. She does more than dress for success—she dresses for eternity. As she "presses through the messes" that life presents to her, she honors her God first.

6.   She had a relationship of dependence on God "She opens her mouth with wisdom, and on her tongue *is* the law of kindness. She watches over the ways of her household, and does not eat the bread of idleness. Her children rise up and call her blessed; her husband *also,* and he praises her: "Many daughters have done well, but you excel them all." Charm *is* deceitful and beauty *is* passing, but a woman *who* fears the Lord, she shall be praised. Give her of the fruit of her hands, and let her own works praise her in the gates" (Proverbs 31:26–31). This "virtuous" woman's #1 quality was: she was saved. As a practicing believer, she lived her life in a manner that pleased/honored the Lord (she took God seriously and placed a high value on her relationship with Him). How did Lemuel (Solomon) describe this woman? She was right in what she said (Proverbs 31:26). From Proverbs 1:2, what was Solomon's goal in writing this book? He wanted to find the "wisdom" that Solomon sought in Proverbs 31:26. What Solomon looked for in the previous 31 chapters of Proverbs was now looking him in the face in the person of this virtuous woman of Proverbs 31:10–31. How did this woman use her tongue? Did she use her voice for profanity or gossip? No, she taught her children the Law/Word of the Lord. For what was she respected (Proverbs 31:27–28)? She was respected for what she saw (Proverbs 31:27–28). She set her eyes on other people's needs with compassionate consideration. What did she get in response? She was rewarded with praise. Her daughters said, "When we grow up, we want to be just like her." Then, what was her reputation (Proverbs 31:29–31)? She was a super mother, wife, woman, and, as a multi-tasker, she excelled all others in her work performance and ethics (Proverbs 31:29). She was

a spiritual lady—her beauty was not skin deep, it went all the way to her heart (Proverbs 31:30).[103] She was splendid in everything she was and in all she tried to do (Proverbs 31:31). Like her husband, she too was praised at the city gate. It is never too late to say, "I love you, Mom. Thanks for being you!" Praise the Lord for all the excellent and virtuous women in our world who do more than raise children—they bring them to God. No government program, day care, school, nanny, or father can ever take the place of a godly mom. Thank God that Solomon's virtuous woman is personified as wisdom in the thirty-one chapters of Proverbs where God said, "Seek wisdom." A mother who shares God's wisdom greatly improves her children's spiritual health. If you are a husband or a father, praise God if/when your wife personifies the wisdom that Solomon sought in the chapters of Proverbs. Isn't it interesting that this book of Proverbs, in which Solomon seeks wisdom, culminates with Solomon's discovery of wisdom that breathes, lives, and moves?

Key questions (from Ecclesiastes 1:2 and Proverbs 1–31):[104]

Is it possible, in part, that Solomon wrote the book of Ecclesiastes out of regret, in his own eyes, for being a failed national leader and, in God's eyes, for being a failure as a parent? Could Solomon have been a more successful parent if he had invested more time in the life of his son (it was during Rehoboam's reign that the ten northern tribes rebelled against Solomon's son's leadership and divided the kingdom)? Yes or No: Are there Proverbs and other scripture passages that parents can apply when their children fail to live up to a parent's hopes or God's expectations? If so, make a list of the passages. From Proverbs 1:2–4, list and discuss ten reasons why God gave children parents (list ten parental responsibilities, as given by God, and how you—as a parent—are fulfilling them). In what ways can a parent teach his/her child to "take God seriously" and "fear the Lord" (see Proverbs 1:7–9)? From Proverbs 1:10–16, since peer groups can influence your child to engage in spiritually negative activities and live a life that does not please God, what responsibilities do parents have concerning their child's peer groups (can a parent invite his/her child's peer groups over to the house for activities, meals, or other events, or is parental engagement with a child's peer group "off limits")? From Proverbs 2:1–5, Joshua 1:6–8), since God's estimation of success is based on the knowledge of God's Word and its application into life, what should parents counsel their children to do in order for their children to obtain the knowledge and wisdom that will help them live their lives in a manner that honors the Lord (review the three recommendations made in the study on Proverbs 2:1–5)? Since a child who embraces parental discipline and God's Word is promised a longer life of increased quality, what should the child embrace and what can the child avoid in order to experience a longer life and a better quality of life (see Proverbs 3:1–6)? From Proverbs 3:5–6, make a list of "your part" and make a separate list defining "God's part" in the "trust," "lean," and "acknowledge" aspects of relying on God for guidance. What kind of an attitude adjustment is required in the life of a child if he/she appears to be "on the path" to "wasting" the parental discipline he/she receives as a child (see Proverbs 3:11–12)? As it relates to Solomon's teachings in Proverbs 3:21–26, explain the "V" illustration (mentioned in the endnote) as it applies to the lifelong consequences of the "bad decisions" a person might make as a child. As implied in Proverbs 4:1–9, when you were young what "bad" advice did your parents give you that you are not/will not give to your children and what "good" advice did your parents give you that you will pass down to your children? How does a child's obedience add to the quality and quantity of a child's life (see Proverbs 4:10–13, 20–23)? In what ways does a child's immoral relationships—both physical and online—affect the future quality of a child's life (see Proverbs 5:1–8, 20, 1 Corinthians 15:33)? What is the disadvantage of cosigning for a grown child's loan (see Proverbs 6:1–5, 20–23)? In what ways can a parent warn his/her children to "not repeat" the mistakes the parent made when that parent was in his/her "growing up" years (see Proverbs 7:1–3, 24–27)? What is the importance of a parent or a child keeping his/her "spiritual commitments current" (see Proverbs 8:1–4, 32)? Since every child's work ethic is a self-portrait of his/her soul, discuss the truths Solomon shared concerning laziness, when found in a child (see Proverbs 10:1, 5, Proverbs 6:7,:9; 10:5, 26; 12:24–27; 13:4; 18:9; 19:15, 24; 20:4; 21:25–26; 22:13; 24:10). How should a parent deal with his/her child when that child is a "scoffer" who merely humors his/her parent rather than a child who honors his/her parent in the Lord (see Proverbs 13:1, 14)? As a parent, what is the value of, every time possible, being "stronger than" his/her child's "strongest moment" (see Proverbs 13:24)? Describe ways that you, as a parent, can make your home a "safe place" for your child (see Proverbs 14:26–27)? Discuss this principle: "When children "get their way" when they are young, they will walk in "their own way" when they are older" (see Proverbs 15:20, 32). As implied in Proverbs 17:2, in what ways will the negative patterns children establish while they are young come back to haunt them when they become adults? As a man with potentially hundreds of children, why did Solomon imply that grandchildren were the "joy" of grandparents (see Proverbs 17:6)? Describe a "spoiled" child, the reasons the child is "spoiled," and what can be done to change the legacy an unrepentant "spoiled" child will leave behind (see Proverbs 17:21, 25, 28). Since parents must "parent together," develop and define a "philosophy of parenting" of which both of you agree (see Proverbs 19:13, 18, 20, 25–27, 29). What is the difference between your child living a life that is "character driven" rather than a life that is "emotion led" (see Proverbs 20:7)? How should a parent deal with a child who "talks back to" his/her parent and what are the consequences of a child who continues to disrespect his/her parents (see Proverbs 20:20–21)? Make a list of the various ways that God will reward the life of a child who lives a life of faithfulness to God (see Proverbs 20:27, 29–30). In detail, principle by principle, explain the truths presented in Proverbs 22:1, 6. As implied in Proverbs 22:28 and Proverbs 23:10–11, define some boundaries that a parent should establish for his/her child—in the areas of behavior, morality, purity, companionships, friendships, and other vital areas of life. In what ways does a child's biblical discipline benefit the child when he/she is older (see Proverbs 23:13–14 with 22:15)? Emotionally and in other ways, what is the parental response to a child who obeys as compared to when a child disobeys (see Proverbs 23:22–28)? Other than the voice/influence of the parent, what other voices—in society—vie for your child's attention (see Proverbs 24:21–22)? Knowing of Solomon's lack of success in raising his son, Rehoboam, describe Solomon's parental pain (see Proverbs 27:11). In what ways are children like lambs who need to be shepherded (see Proverbs 27:23–24)? Discuss the following statement: The stings of a child's unwise actions can leave permanent scars on the hearts of his/her parents (Proverbs 28:7). How can a parent "build trust" with his/her child (see Proverbs 28:24)? When a child "hardens" his/her neck (heart) to a parent's discipline, what blessings will God remove from that child's life (see Proverbs 29:1–3)? In understanding that it is never too late to start parenting correctly, are you a parent or a "(s)parent" (see Proverbs 29:15, 17, 21)? In your family, who or what establishes the guidelines for raising your children—God or society (see Proverbs 30:1, 11–15)? As a parent, what safeguards do you establish, in your home, to prevent society's predators from targeting your children (see Proverbs 30:17)? Since, if you want your children to walk in the ways of the Lord,—as a parent—you need to walk in God's ways yourself, what intentional actions do you take to model Christianity in your home (see Proverbs 31:1–3)? From Proverbs 31:10–31, define the role of a godly mother (establish a list of qualities that characterize a virtuous woman).

Notes:

How to Raise an Abel When the World is Raising Cain

Biblical Principles for Parenting

As we observe society, believers become painfully aware that our world is largely populated by people who live their lives as if God does not exist, raise their children to exist apart from the influence and authority of God, and, as a result, are disappointed when their children do not live up to the parents' original expectations. Is it possible that, among other reasons, in beginning his book of Ecclesiastes with the name "Abel" (Vanity/Emptiness/Futility), that Solomon wrote Ecclesiastes from the perspective of a parent who was expressing his frustrations at raising the son whom Solomon described in Proverbs (Rehoboam) as a child who more resembled Adam and Eve's Cain than he did resemble Adam and Eve's Abel—an Abel who (thankfully) did not live up to the meaning of his name and instead became a man whom God blessed (see Hebrews 11:4).[105]

If Adam and Eve had it to do over again, how would they parent? In their do-over, what would they change? Would they parent differently? What principles would they follow if they were raising their children today? With these questions in mind, let us ask a question that applies to parents today: How do believers—who want to parent "God's way"—parent by the Book?

From selected scriptures, here are a few ideas:

1. Whether prior to the Fall or after man's Fall into sin, God wants families to have children—biologically or through adoption (Genesis 1:28–29, 9:1).

In the context of forming the earth through creation, God commanded Adam and Eve to "be fruitful and multiply; [and] fill (replenish) the earth" (Genesis 1:28). He repeated that commandment to Noah in Genesis 9:1. Whether prior to the Fall or after man's Fall into sin, God wants families to have children—biologically or through adoption. Since that is the case, how many children should parents have? Since "happy is the man who has his quiver full of them" (see Psalm 127:5) and, since a Hebrew archer's quiver held five arrows, if we, as parents, have/had less than five children, were we "trying hard enough?" Perhaps today, the number of children is not the main objective. Perhaps having children is! In light of the number of abortions that take place in our world, couples who cannot have children naturally may want to "make a statement against abortion" by adopting children instead.[106] Praise God that, in spite of her "pain in childbirth," Eve obeyed God's plan, was "fruitful and multiplied," and had children.

2. You can be included in the fulfillment of God's promise to Abraham in Genesis 12:3 when you and your children form a salvation relationship with Christ (Genesis 12:1–3, Galatians 3:13–29).

In telling Abram (later called Abraham) to leave his country, God made promises. One promise was that, through Abram's offspring, "all the families of the earth shall be blessed" (Genesis 12:3). Through Whom was this promise fulfilled? Jesus Christ. How can a person experience this promise? If you would like to be part of the fulfillment of a biblical prophecy, become a part of Abraham's spiritual "seed (offspring)" by receiving Jesus Christ as Savior. Understanding this, the central focus of Genesis 12:1–3 is not Abram, but Jesus. Be family with God. If you have not done it before, join His family today by receiving Christ as Savior. As a parent, make sure that you introduce your child to a saving knowledge of Christ at the earliest possible age. On a personal note, every day—when they were young—my wife and I prayed that our children would receive Christ as soon as they were able and become practicing believers. Then, when they were older and saved, we prayed that they would marry "good, strong Christians who were practicing believers who have ministries and lead people to Christ." Now, we pray for any grandchildren that they might receive Christ at the earliest possible age and become practicing believers. Praise God! He answers prayer!

3. One of God's commanded purposes for parents is that dad and mom would "keep (guard like a sentinel) the way of the Lord [and] do righteousness (practice biblically consistent right living) and [live justly before the Lord]" (Genesis 18:19).

Why did God give children parents? One of God's commanded purposes for parents is that dad and mom would "keep (guard like a sentinel) the way of the Lord [and] do righteousness (practice biblically consistent right living) and [live justly before the Lord]" (Genesis 18:19). Since people become what they choose, the child of God—who wants to be blessed—needs to choose the pathway of the Lord. It is much easier for the child to choose that pathway when the parents themselves are living actively for the Lord. Model commitment to Christ. Put a "padlock on your wedlock" and keep your spiritual commitments current for the Lord.

4. Parenting requires sacrifice (Genesis 22:1–14, Hebrews 11:17–19).

Parenting requires sacrifice. Realizing that God always gives believers His best, Christian parents must give to God what is most precious to them: their children. To do that, the parents must trust God to give back His best to them. Consider Abraham when he took his child Isaac to be offered to God at Moriah (see Genesis 22). What was going through father Abraham's mind? Was he thinking, "God gave me this child. Will God now take this child away? If He does, will God replace Isaac with another child, by grace?" Although ultimate sacrifices are never easy, God can do more with our child's life than we can. Everyone has an Isaac whom we would rather keep for ourselves. Give your Isaac to God. When you do, both the parents and the child will be blessed.

5. Because God plays no favorites, neither should we—especially in the home (Genesis 37:1–2, 1 Samuel 16:1–15, Acts 10:34, Romans 2:11, Proverbs 28:21).

As a parent, do you have a favorite child? If so, does that favoritism add to the relationship or subtract from it? What does favoritism destroy? In Genesis 37:1–2, a father of twelve sons and one daughter played favorites. It fostered bitterness, promoted jealousy, and bore its fruit in resentment, rejection, and remorse. Yet, God used Jacob's favoritism toward Joseph to redirect His child into the next phase of God's will (saving the world from famine). In 1 Samuel 16:7, a father of eight sons played favorites. Judging his sons by society's values, which include outward appearance, academics, abilities, affluence, and accomplishments, the father promoted the seven at the expense of the one. But God "sees not as a man sees … God looks on the heart" (1 Samuel 16:7). God chose David. At the foot of the cross, God plays no favorites. Everyone is equal to Him. All can come to Christ, by grace through faith (Ephesians 2:8–9). All can serve Him (Ephesians 2:10). Because God plays no favorites, neither should we—especially in the home (Acts 10:34, Romans 2:11, Proverbs 28:21).

6. The worst that is offered by Christ is better than the best society has to offer (Exodus 2:1–10, Hebrews 11:10, 23–29).

Is God powerless in a world that rejects God's truths and denies the existence of God? What is the role of the parent in raising a child who will practice belief when that child becomes an adult? Knowing that children become adults, do parents have an obligation to raise their children with a view toward how God will use them in the future? Consider Abraham. Unlike Lot, Abraham looked beyond what his surroundings and culture had to offer and "waited for the city which has foundations, whose builder and maker is God" (Hebrews 11:10). Consider the life of Moses: even as a youth, Moses focused on God. As a child, Moses understood that it is not who we are in relation to popularity, power, or possessions. What matters is this: Whose we are—we belong to Jesus. In spite of living in the palace, as "next-in-line" for Egypt's throne, Moses prioritized God. If Moses had not "ordered his priorities," other than a few archeologists or Egyptologists, how many twenty-first century people would even know his name? The worst that is offered by Christ is better than the best of our personal Egypts (Hebrews 11:23–29).

7.　The greatest blessing a child can have is godly parents (Exodus 20:1–5, 34:6–7; Numbers 14:18; Malachi 4:4–6).

The greatest blessing a child can have is godly parents. Since children become reflections of their parents (most children do what parents do more than they do what parents say), parents must realize that they have a profound effect on the future of their children, their children's children, and beyond (Exodus 20:1–5, 34:6–7, Numbers 14:18). Put another way, although you cannot do anything about your ancestors, you can have an impact on your descendants. Because nations are built child by child, the world's future is dependent on proper parenting in the home. Having a godly child is a privilege. Being a godly parent is a responsibility given by the Lord. Be a godly parent. Because, one day, your child will become "you," let your focus be committed faithfulness to the Lord.

8.　Since, in the home, more is caught than taught, be a "priority" parent. Parent "incarnationally," by "living out" Jesus in what you do, where you go, what you say, and how you respond to life (Deuteronomy 6:4–9, 11:19; Psalm 128:1–4; Judges 2:10).

As parents, how obvious is your Christianity? Do you live (practice) authentic Christianity before your children when you rise up in the morning, meet to eat during the day, when you are carpooling to school, and, publicly, have you put your relationship with Christ between your children's eyes and wear it on your sleeve (Deuteronomy 6:4–9)? In what ways and how often do you let your children know that they do not belong to the world—they belong to Jesus? Other than the times you *talk* about Jesus, can your children *see* Jesus in you? Is your daily Christianity genuine and real (Deuteronomy 11:19)? Does your table talk center on the Lord (Deuteronomy 6:4–9, Psalm 128:1–4)? Is Christ your life (everywhere you go) or is your relationship with Jesus merely a means to heaven, having no real impact on the testimony of your daily life? Since, in the home, more is caught than taught, are you discipling your children for Christ or merely raising your children to be "good citizens" and "successful" in society? Since what you *really* are is who you are in the home, how would your children describe you *spiritually*? Since children are more likely to find a Father in God when they find something of God in their father (Psalm 128:1–4), parent with a purpose. Be a "priority" parent. Parent "incarnationally" by "living out" Jesus in what you do, where you go, what you say, and how you respond to life. Provide biblical instruction in the home. Invest time with your family. Provide an environment where your children can grow. Nurture your children in the Lord. Model the Christ-life before them, by working out what Christ works in. Tell your child, "I love you," with your actions as well as your voice. Be merciful. Show grace. Remember that your child is a child and not yet an adult (treat them accordingly). Make your child your friend (Titus 2:4). Sacrifice for your family. Cultivate a relationship of mutual respect and mutual love. Influence the people who influence your child. Be transparent and real. Show compassion. Truly care. Refuse to frustrate your child. Trust God: first, last, and always. Understand that you, as the parent, are the difference-maker in the spiritual, social, emotional, and psychological progress/development of your child. With your child, read the Bible. Pray. Have regular devotions—privately and with the family. Include God as an active member in your home—in your conversations and in your commitments to each other. In the presence of your children, have a "testimony" and not a "testi-phony," and your children will see Jesus in you (1 Thessalonians 2:7–9).

9.   As your children get older, come to grips with the fact that, as you did when you were younger, they will too—they will leave the home (Deuteronomy 32:11–12a; Genesis 2:24, 12:1–2; Matthew 19:5; John 3:16–17; Ephesians 5:31).

In all probability, the phrase "empty nester" finds its source in Deuteronomy 32:11–12a where the mother eagle "encouraged" her baby eaglets to "spread their wings" and leave the nest. In observing this time of transition in the lives of a parent's offspring, Moses wrote, "As an eagle stirs up its nest, hovers over its young, spreading out its wings, taking them up, [and] carrying them on its wings, *So* the Lord ..." (Deuteronomy 32:11–12a). "As an eagle ... so the Lord." Concerning the Lord, what was His commandment to Adam and Eve and to their children? God said, "Be fruitful and multiply [and] fill (replenish) the earth" (Genesis 1:28). A couple's offspring cannot "fill the [entire] earth" without leaving home to do it.[107] To reinforce this truth, God added, "Therefore a man shall leave his father and mother and be joined to his wife, and they shall become one flesh" (Genesis 2:24). "Leave" is the Hebrew term *azab*, which speaks of "letting go and leaving behind." "Joined" is the Hebrew term *dabaq*, which means to "cleave or stick like glue." It is the same term inspired scripture used, in Psalm 137:6, of a person's tongue "cleaving/sticking" to the roof of a person's mouth (if you have ever spread peanut butter on one slice of bread and put it in your mouth with the wrong side up, you experienced the word *cleave*). It was used, in Psalm 102:5, of bones cleaving to a [malnourished] person's skin (our hearts sympathize with all who have similar desperate needs). It was used in Ruth 1:14 of Ruth's relationship with Naomi where the daughter-in-law Ruth said, "Where you go, I will go and where you die, I will die" (eventually Ruth, in Ruth 4, did leave Naomi and established her own home, apart from her mother-in-law, Naomi, with her kinsman-redeemer husband Boaz). In addition, this term *cleave* was used in Joshua 22:5 of Israel's "Conquest of Canaan" loyalty to God (as God never forsakes us, we should never forsake Him); in Daniel 2:43 of Nebuchadnezzar's toes in his golden image (his toes refused to cleave one to another—there was no "toe jam" there); in 1 Kings 22:34 of the soldering in the joints of armor (holes in the armor were opportunities for the enemy to attack); and, in the passage I like best, in Job 38:38, where dirt clods cleave together as one. Have you ever seen a dirt clod? Growing up, my friends and I would cross the street to an old construction site and, as boys did in those days, we had dirt clod fights (all of us were baseball players—pitchers and catchers—with "live" arms, which meant that, when we were throwing the dirt clods, it was fortunate for us. But, when we were on the receiving end of those dirt clods, it was unfortunate for us). Left in their original condition, those dirt clods hurt! But when God added a little rainwater, the dirt clods got soft, and, soaked in water, they "blended together" as one to the point that, together as one, none could tell the difference between one dirt clod and another. Do not be offended, but what is one (potential) description of marriage? In applying Job 38:38 to wedded bliss, it is merely "two clods coming together as one." That description may not be flattering, but, in marriage, when a couple adds the water of God's Word, God takes two pieces of clay, blends them together, and makes them one. Inseparable, as two "clods" formed into one, the man and the woman are now a new unit dedicated to God and applying all of the guidelines for marriage included in scripture. One of those guidelines is to form a home apart from dad and mom—with separate headship and, if possible, a separate residence (see Genesis 12:1–2, Matthew 19:5, John 3:16–17, Ephesians 5:31). "As the eagle … so the Lord?" Before a mother eagle kicks her eaglets "out of the nest" the eaglets are comfortable, cared for, and content. Then, suddenly, still loving her offspring, the mother eagle upsets the eaglets' peaceful setting emotionally, physically, and in other ways and pushes her eaglets—one after another—over the edge of the nest.[108] "But I am scared! I cannot fly!" For perhaps the first time in its life, the eaglet flaps its wings yet drops like lead heading toward the ground. But the mother eagle, caring for her young, swoops down and catches the eaglet on her back, rescuing the eaglet from danger. This same scenario is repeated again and again until the eaglet's wings "catch wind," and the now flying eaglet soars into the sky—autonomous and independent of the mother, yet encouraged by its parent (exchanging its former fears and weaknesses for new-found strength)—and, using "wing power" supplied by God, the eaglet rises above its circumstances and does what every eaglet has done before it—it establishes its own identity.[109] Both empty nesters and their children experience a myriad of emotions when children leave the home. Yet, at the appropriate time, leaving the home is a vital part of God's plan for mankind to "be fruitful and multiply [and] fill/ replenish the earth" (see Genesis 2:24). Praise God that He bears us "on eagle's wings" and brings us to Himself (see Exodus 19:4). God cares for His own, regardless of our situation.

10. There is no greater joy in parenting than to know that your life's investment in your children's lives resulted in "service for the Savior" (Joshua 24:15, Isaiah 54:13, and 3 John 4).

Mrs. Joshua must have been pleased with her husband when he stood before God's people and said, "Choose for yourselves this day whom you will serve … but as for me *and my house(hold)*, *we* will serve the Lord" (Joshua 24:15). There is no greater joy in parenting than to know that your life's investment in your children's lives resulted in "service for the Savior" (3 John 4). Pray daily for your children that they will grow strong in the grace and knowledge of Jesus Christ our Lord ("grace" in who they are and "knowledge" in what they know and in what they do for Christ). Then, because prayer disarms principalities, unleashes God's power, defeats the devil, takes down strongholds, and helps to free your child from sin's shackles, praise God ahead of time for answered prayer that results in service to the King (see Ephesians 6:11–12 and 1 Corinthians 10:4–5).

11. The greatest calling any woman can have is motherhood (1 Samuel 1–2; Judges 13:2–5, 24–25; 2 Peter 1:8; Psalm 113:9; Jeremiah 1:5).

The greatest calling any woman can have is motherhood. Knowing that God would love her whether she had a child or not (2 Peter 1:8 teaches that it is *spiritual* barrenness and not *physical* barrenness that grieves a holy God), Hannah prayed for a son (1 Samuel 1:10–11). When God answered her prayer, she returned her son to the Lord (1 Samuel 1:20). That son (Samuel) became one of the greatest leaders in the history of his nation (1 Samuel 1–25). God has a plan for every believer's life (Jeremiah 1:5). Since having children is rarely about the parent and always about God, each parent must do more than pray *for* a child. The parent must pray that each child will be what God wants that child to become. As a believing parent, the next time you look at your child, see that child as living evidence that believers have a God Who hears and answers prayer. He is the God Who "settles the childless woman in her home as a happy mother of children" (Psalm 113:9). Praise the Lord!

12. Since godly parents can have ungodly children, if parents "start early" and "stay balanced"—if parents discipline their children early, often, and in a balanced manner, and, if believing parents do not neglect their children—through indifference—but instead enact "discipline that disciples," their children will be a blessing to them in old age (1 Samuel 2:12, 17; 2 Samuel 12:24, 14:28, 15:10; 2 Samuel 13; 1 Kings 1–2; Proverbs 1:8–9, 13:24, 23:13–14, 29:15, 17; Luke 15:11–32; Hebrews 12:6).

Sometimes godly parents can have ungodly children (the sons of Eli: 1 Samuel 2:12, 17; the children of David: 2 Samuel 13 with 1 Kings 1–2; and the prodigal son: Luke 15:11–32). In examining the three Bible families mentioned, what do we find?

A. The family of Eli (see 1 Samuel 2:12–36): The tabernacle priest Eli spent so much of his time and energy ministering to other families and to their children that he neglected his own. In contrast to Hannah's son, Samuel—who was raised also in the tabernacle at the same time as Eli's sons—Hophni and Phinehas were corrupt, dishonest, and immoral (see 1 Samuel 2:12, 13–17, 22). Refusing to honor God (refusing to place a "high value" on God), God refused to honor both the sons and their household (see 1

Samuel 2:30–36 with a special emphasis on 1 Samuel 2:30b). Concerning the prodigal (see Luke 15:11-32), parents can raise their children right and the children can still go wrong. In addition, concerning the older son, a child does not have to leave the farm in order to leave the father. Since God rewards for faithfulness, He will reward parents who invest time and pour love into the lives of their children (see Romans 12:3).

B. Concerning David's sons:

1. In 1 Samuel 12:1–23 with 1 Samuel 13:1–21, in all probability, one son, Amnon, expected society to condemn his father for David's sin of immorality (adultery) with/against Uriah's wife, Bathsheba. Yet, in the public's eye—aside from the prophet Nathan who did condemn David's sin (see 1 Samuel 12:1–23), David got a "pass." He suffered little "public consequence." David remained the king. Perceiving a "lack of immediate or public consequences for sin," just as David took another man's wife (Uriah's wife, Bathsheba), Amnon took another man's sister (Absalom's sister, Tamar). It was a sin that cost Amnon his life (just as David had Bathsheba's husband Uriah killed at the gate of Ammon—see 1 Samuel 11:1, 14–21—a second son of David, Absalom, removed "the threat in his life" by murdering his stepbrother, Amnon). Like father, like son?[110]

2. As David's sons stood in the shadows—feeling neglected and standing somewhere behind the palace court's curtains—their father invested as many moments, in as many days possible, in ruling his political kingdom (see 2 Kings 1–2).[111] In the context of their father's death, what motivated two of David's sons (Adonijah and Absalom) to make a power grab for David's kingdom? Perhaps, as they watched their dad place a higher priority on his job than he did on his family, David's indifference to his sons motivated Adonijah and Absalom to remove the one obstacle/object in their lives that stood between them and a proper "parent-child" relationship with their father—David's throne. Since God and family must be a parent's "top two" priorities (in that sequential order), as a parent, what attracts your attention away from your children and in what do you invest your time, apart from the time spent with your family? What misplaced priorities and "outside-the-home/other-than-family" focuses rob you of a better/stronger relationship with your children? Is your distraction your job, other people, pleasure, entertainment, "screen" time, your adult friends, recreation, "me" time, the "busy-ness" of life, or some other substitute that keeps you from building a "lifetime relationship" with the son(s) or daughter(s) with whom God has blessed your life? Most parents have eighteen years only to build lifetime relationships with their children. If your focus has been misplaced, take advantage of the time you have remaining. Establish a foundation of faith, be

a "priority parent," and build a lasting and impenetrably solid relationship with the most precious people in your life: your marriage partner and your children.

C. Concerning the prodigal son in Luke 15:11–24: How did he become a prodigal (what contributed to the prodigal believing that he was entitled to his father's inheritance—now—even though his father had not yet died)? In what way(s) do modern parents merely give their children what they want instead of what they need? What about the elder brother in Luke 15:25–31 (is it possible to leave the father while never leaving the farm)? To the father's credit, because he cherished his father-son relationship, he forgave, blessed the son (the repentant prodigal) whose heart was right with him, and, by running out to meet him, the father let his son know that wherever he's been and whatever he's done, we have a Father Who desperately wants His children home.

D. In general, using the texts cited above, here are several thoughts about the upbringing and discipline of children. One reason that "children do not turn out as expected" may be that (s)parents who refuse to participate in their children's spiritual development will reap what they sow. Since parents have a responsibility in "shaping their child's will," as your child grows, refuse to be like Eli and David. Instead address every action, "incident," and response in your child's life. If the action, "incident," or response is good: praise the child. If the action, "incident," or response is inconsistent with God's biblical expectations, be "stronger than your child's strongest moment" and discipline your child, in love (Hebrews 12:6). Child discipline may hurt you in a different place (your heart) than it does your child (see Proverbs 13:24, 23:13–14, 29:15, 17), but, if parents "start early" and "stay balanced"—if parents discipline their children early, often, and in a balanced manner, and, if believing parents do not neglect their children through indifference but instead enact "discipline that disciples," their children will be a blessing to them in old age (Psalm 113:9, 128:1–6; Proverbs 31:28; Isaiah 54:13, 6:1–3).

13. God gave parents children to raise for the Lord, release back to God, and become sanctuaries for Jesus (Psalm 127:1–5, 139:13–16, 128:1–4).

Have you ever received a gift and felt bad when you returned it or exchanged it at a store? There is one gift that God says is okay to "Return to Sender." That gift is your child, given as a heritage ("gift") from the Lord (Psalm 127:3, Genesis 33:5). Fearfully and wonderfully made by the hand of God Himself and fashioned by the master craftsman in the womb (Psalm 139:13–16), God gave parents children to raise for the Lord, release back to God, and become sanctuaries for Jesus (1 Corinthians 6:19–20). With that in mind, God wants each parent's quiver full. Since an Israelite quiver held five arrows, it has been said that if you have less than five children, you are not trying hard enough! By the way, since those "olive plants" around your table are identified as "arrows" (see

Psalm 127:4), is it accurate to say that children should be shot? In the arena of child discipline, think of that concept in these terms: if you keep the bowstring of your child(ren)'s correction loose, your arrow (child/children) will fall by the wayside and fail to reach God's desired goal. If the bowstring of your discipline is too tight, your bow (that's you) will break (your children will wear you out). But if the bowstring of your corrective measures is just right and properly balanced, your arrows (your children) will hit the target that God wants them to achieve. So, if you ever feel like "shooting" your "arrows" (your children), be biblical and stay balanced!

14. Since children are like "wet cement," just as a child left to himself/herself will be bent in the direction of the influence he/she receives from peer groups and society, a child bent toward Christ will practice biblical values when he/she is "old" (Proverbs 1:1–7, 3:1–6, 22:1–6; 1 Peter 2:2–3).

Are children like wet cement? Are they imprinted-for-life with what they see, what they hear, and where they go? If so, what should a parent do? God's manual on parenting says: teach your child to take God seriously (Proverbs 1:1–7). Teach your child to trust in God (Proverbs 3:5–6). And train your child biblically, in "the way he should go [so that] when he is old, he will not depart from [the pathway of the Lord]" (Proverbs 22:6). As a reminder, to "train" was first used of midwives, who placed grapes or date jam in the roof of a child's mouth or on a baby's gums to develop a taste for the mother's milk (it pictures the parent developing a thirst in the child for the way of the Lord). In Proverbs 22:6, a "child" can describe any offspring living under the parent's roof. It was used of an unborn baby (Judges 13:5–12), a newborn infant (1 Samuel 4:21), an infant still unweaned (1 Samuel 1:22), baby Moses at three months old (Exodus 2:6), preteen Ishmael (Genesis 21:16); Joseph at age seventeen (Genesis 37:2), a young man ready for marriage (Genesis 34:19), and a thirty-year-old living at home (Genesis 41:12, 26). Regardless of the age, as long as a child is living at home, the law of parenting is "my roof, my rules." A "way" is a distinctive characteristic, manner of living, or way a baby is "bent." It is the way of an eagle as it soars, the way of a serpent as it slithers on the ground, the way of a ship as it cuts the waves (Proverbs 30:18–19), and the way of an archer as he shoots an arrow (Proverbs 7:12, Psalm 127:4–5). As is the twig, so grows the tree. What a child learns in his/her youth, he/she never forgets. A child left to himself/herself will be bent in the direction of the influence he/she receives from peer groups and society. But a child whose parents bend that child toward Christ will practice biblical values when he/she is "old" (in Proverbs 22:6, "old" makes reference to the age when a boy first grows a beard: age fourteen). Must teenagers go astray? According to Proverbs 22:6, no! It is never too late to lovingly "bend" your child toward God. Why wait for society to "get" your child? Lead your household to saving faith at the earliest possible age (Acts 16:31). Bend your child toward the Lord. Nurture your children for Christ. Start early (1 Peter 2:2–3). Start today!

15. All lives are sacred, including the little "yet-to-be-born" lives in the womb waiting to be delivered. (Micah 6:7; Judges 11:30–40; Psalm 139:13–16; Jeremiah 1:5).

Have you ever known a parent to sacrifice his/her child on the altar of society's values—commonly called the world (2 Kings 21:6; 2 Chronicles 28:1–4; Jeremiah 19:5–12, 32:35–36)? Jephthah sacrificed his child (Judges 11). But his sacrifice was in honor of God and did not cost his child her life (Judges 11:38–39). Abraham (Genesis 22) was ordered by God to sacrifice his child. But God spared the child by providing a ram, picturing the resurrection of Jesus Christ (Hebrews 11:17–19). Since children are a gift from the Lord, why do so many parents throw them away (Micah 6:7)? Since, in Psalm 139:13–16, God used pronouns acknowledging the "personhood" of an unborn baby ("me, I, my"), why does society consider an unborn baby as a "potential human" rather than as a "human with potential?" If a baby has his/her own body, shouldn't that baby have a choice? Take your child's hand, not your child's life. All lives are sacred, including the little "yet-to-be-born" lives in the womb waiting to be delivered. Praise God that Mary spared Jesus. Thankfully, Joseph recognized adoption as an option and became a father for his Lord (Matthew 1:18–25).

16. The parent's foremost responsibility is to lead his/her child to the Savior (Matthew 10:13–16; 18:2–6, 10; 19:14; Mark 9:36–37; Luke 17:1–2; 2 Timothy 1:5).

What is the primary role of a parent? The parent's foremost responsibility is to lead his/her child to the Savior. Yet, how often are parents guilty of placing obstructions in the pathway that leads to the Lord? Timothy's grandmother, Eunice; his mother, Lois; and his "spiritual father in the faith," Paul, each played a role in leading Timothy to Christ. Children can come to God (2 Chronicles 24:1–2, 34:1–3; Ecclesiastes 12:1; Isaiah 6:1–8, 54:13; Jonah 4:11; Matthew 19:14; Luke 18:15–17; Acts 2:39, 16:31; 2 Timothy 1:5). As soon as a child is old enough to "discern his right hand from his left hand" (Jonah 4:11) and understand that he/she is a sinner, the believing parent should lead that child to the Lord and begin a discipleship ministry in that child's life.[112] Otherwise entire decades of spiritual growth can be lost. Since Jesus demonstrated God's love for children and placed a high value on them by saying, "Suffer [the] little children, and forbid them not (do not hinder them), to come unto me: for of such is the kingdom of heaven" (Matthew 19:14), so should we. We should love each child as Christ loves us and value children as God values His children—both physically and spiritually in the Lord. Then, when your child forms a salvation relationship with Christ, celebrate and rejoice because, once saved, your child will do more than live with you, on earth, for eighteen years. Your child will spend an eternity with you in heaven. How can parents lead their children to Christ so that they form a "salvation relationship" with Christ? After sharing these truths, lead your child to a decision:

1. Admit you're a sinner (Romans 3:10, 23).
2. Recognize that sin deserves eternal punishment (Romans 6:23a).
3. Realize that Jesus experienced sin's punishment for you (Romans 5:6, 8).
4. Respond by applying what Christ did on the cross to your life. Use your words (Romans 10:9–10). Ask Jesus into your life as your personal Savior (John 1:12, Romans 10:13, Titus 3:5–6).
5. Remind your child that "once saved, always saved" (1 John 5:11–13).[113]

17. Right behavior and the child's biblically consistent response to/in the Lord is obedience to dad and mom as both father and mother parent together (Ephesians 6:1–4, Colossians 3:20, Proverbs 1:8–9).

What is right for a child? Right behavior and the child's biblically consistent response to/in the Lord is obedience to dad and mom as both father and mother parent together. Because God honors those who honor Him (1 Samuel 2:30b), through biblical obedience, a child places a "high value" ("honor") on God's delegated (mediatorial) authorities in the home: his/her mom and dad. How does the child benefit by responding with proper obedience, by showing sincere respect, and by placing a high value ("honor") on dad and mom, in the home? God rewards these children with a biblically consistent life quality (Ephesians 6:1–4—"it may be well with you") and with long life on earth (Psalm 90:10—a quantity of years). What does proper parenting look like? It looks like fathers refusing to exasperate (frustrate) their children to the point that the children's emotional responses are "out of control" (Ephesians 6:4, Ephesians 4:32—"wrath"). It looks like both the father and the mother parenting intentionally—equipping their children and training them to take God seriously as the children grow and live their lives. One of the best ways to fulfill God's plan for parenting is to love each other—with unconditional love—as husband and wife before your children in the home (Ephesians 5:25–33).

18. It is the responsibility of both older and younger people to establish a pattern of godliness for other people to follow (1 Timothy 4:12–13; Titus 2:3–5, 5–8; Luke 2:40–52).

Perhaps thinking of Jesus when Christ was twelve and teaching in the temple (Luke 2:40–52), to his son in the faith, Paul wrote, "Let no one despise your youth, but be an example to the believers in word, in conduct, in love, in spirit, in faith, in purity. Till I come, give attention to reading, to exhortation, to doctrine" (1 Timothy 4:12–13). "Despise" was used of sinners "thumbing their noses at" grace (Romans 2:4), of society rejecting authority (2 Peter 2:10), and of adults treating their children with contempt (Matthew 18:10). "Youth" is anyone under forty or of military age (1 Timothy 4:12). "Example" is the root for the English word *type*. It speaks of a pattern for believers to follow. In John 20:25, it is the impression (imprint) left by nails when they are removed from wood. In Acts 7:44, it is used of the blueprint for Israel's temple. In Philippians 3:17, it describes the godly influence of practicing believers in the lives of those they meet. In the context of 1 Timothy 4:12–13, it is the responsibility of both older and younger people to establish a pattern of godliness for other people to follow.[114] What kind of imprint does God want younger believers to have?

1. God wants younger believers to leave a positive impression of speech. In what believers say, Paul wrote, "Let your speech be alway(s) with grace, seasoned with salt, that ye may know how ye ought to answer every man" (Colossians 4:6). Always give a grace response.

2. God wants believers to model a godly pattern of conduct. There are people who profess to know God, but in their works, they deny Him (Titus 1:16). Publicly identify with Jesus.

3. God wants younger believers to practice unconditional love. This is accomplished when young people love what God loves, hate what God hates, stick like glue to that which is good, and choose right friends (Romans 12:9–10).

4. God wants younger believers to be excited and passionate about Jesus. Paul admonished his son in the faith Timothy to "fan into flame the spiritual gift (of service) that is in you" (2 Timothy 1:6). Experience revival. Keep the torch of your spiritual testimony and commitment burning. Rekindle a spiritual fire for Christ.

5. In everything and in every way, be faithful to Jesus Christ. "Flee [evil] … Follow after righteousness (biblically consistent living) … Fight the good fight of faith (faithfulness), lay hold on eternal life [unto which] you are called" (see 1 Timothy 6:1–12). Be a change agent for Jesus and fight the fight worth fighting.

6. Be set apart from sin and model biblical values in the things you stand for and in the things you stand against (1 Peter 1:15–16). In addition, study the scriptures. Motivate others. Both know and apply the truths of God's Word (1 Timothy 4:13). When you do, you will both profit personally (individually prosper) and be a positive influence on others who witness your positive testimony for God (1 Timothy 4:15–16). Since your example is an impression, honor your calling. Allow your life to resemble the character qualities of Christ.

General Douglas MacArthur was a famous American hero in the Pacific theater during World War II. In a prayer for his son, in part, MacArthur wrote, "Build me a son, O Lord … [so I can say] … I have not lived in vain."

When it comes to parenting, no one is perfect. But all can be faithful to God. Since the best use of life is to invest it in someone who outlasts you, be the parent that God called you to be for *His* children. Allow your children to see a reflection of Christ in you. Parent for the Lord!

See Galatians 2:20 (Not I, But Christ).

Key questions (from selected scriptures):[115]

In modern times—biologically or through adoption—how can believing parents fulfill God's command to Adam and Eve to "be fruitful and multiply" (Genesis 1:28–29, 9:1)? From Genesis 12:1–3 with Galatians 3:13–29, how can you, as a parent, be part of the fulfillment of God's promise to Abraham that through Abraham's "spiritual offspring" "all the families of the earth shall be blessed" (Genesis 12:3)? Why did God give children parents (Genesis 18:19)? What sacrifices does parenting require—physically, spiritually, mentally, vocationally, geographically, financially, psychologically, emotionally, and in other ways (Genesis 22:1–14, Hebrews 11:17–19)? What are the advantages and/or disadvantages of showing favoritism to one or more of your children? Is it ever appropriate to favor one child over another (Genesis 37:1–2, 1 Samuel 16:1–15, Acts 10:34, Romans 2:11, Proverbs 28:21)? Knowing that children become adults, do parents have an obligation to raise their children with a view toward how God will use them in the future (Exodus 2:1–10, Hebrews 11:10, 23–29)? Since the greatest blessing a child can have is to have godly parents and since, in the home, "more is caught than taught," in what ways are you, as a parent, "working on" being a more godly parent—in private and in public (Exodus 20:1–5, 34:6–7; Numbers 14:18; Malachi 4:4–6)? As a parent, how obvious is your Christianity? Other than the times you talk about Jesus, can your children see Jesus in you in the morning when you get up, as you drive your child to school, in the evenings when everyone is home, and on the weekends when everyone is "merely being themselves" (Deuteronomy 6:4–9, Deuteronomy 11:19, Psalm 128:1–4, Judges 2:10)? Describe the emotions of both the parents and their children when the children "leave the nest" (see Deuteronomy 32:11–12a; Genesis 2:24, 12:1–2; Matthew 19:5; John 3:16–17; Ephesians 5:3). Since your children will, more than likely, become "you" one day, what do they see in you today that they should be like and that they should not be like (Joshua 24:15, Isaiah 54:13, and 3 John 4)? Since having children is rarely about the parent and always about God—beyond prayer—what must each parent do for their children (1 Samuel 1–2; Judges 13:2–5, 24–25; 2 Peter 1:8; Psalm 113:9; Jeremiah 1:5)? Since even godly parents can have ungodly children, what must you do, as a parent, to help your child change the spiritual direction of his/her life? Are you a parent or a "(s)parent" (1 Samuel 2:12, 17; 2 Samuel 12:24, 14:28, 15:10; 2 Samuel 13 with 1 Kings 1–2; Proverbs 1:8–9, 13:24, 23:13–14, 29:15, 17; Luke 15:11–32; Hebrews 12:6)? In the context of raising your child for the Lord and, picturing child-raising as an archer with a bow (see Psalm 127:4), describe ways that your child should be "shot" (Psalm 127:1–5, 139:13–16. and 128:1–4). In what ways are children like "wet cement" (Proverbs 1:1–7, 3:1–6, 22:1–6; 1 Peter 2:2–3)? On which of society's altars do modern-day parents sacrifice their children? In how many ways do believing parents do the same (Micah 6:7, Judges 11:30–40, Psalm 139:13–16, Jeremiah 1:5)? What are the primary roles of a parent as each seeks to develop his/her child physically, spiritually, mentally, vocationally, geographically, financially, psychologically, emotionally, and in other ways (Matthew 10:13–16, 18:2–6, 18:10, 19:14; Mark 9:36–37; Luke 17:1–2; 2 Timothy

1:5)? How does the child benefit by responding with proper obedience, by showing sincere respect, and by placing a high value (honor) on dad and mom in the home (Ephesians 6:1–4, Colossians 3:20, Proverbs 1:8–9)? Make a list of the ways a child or teenager can be a spiritual example to others (see 1 Timothy 4:12–13, Luke 2:40–52). Add to that list the responsibilities of older women and older men toward passing down godly values to younger women and girls and younger men and boys (see Titus 2:3–5, 5–8).

Notes:

Principles for Parenting

1. It is common for parents to expect great things from their children (Genesis 4:1).
2. God establishes the number of children each couple should have (Genesis 4:2, 5:3–5).
3. God wants His children to honor Him (Genesis 4:3–5a).
4. Children can "turn away from" and "turn aside from" the Truth (2 Timothy 4:3–4).
5. Children who depart from the faith do not live a Christ-like life (Jude 4). They are ungodly.
6. Children who depart from the faith make a disgrace of grace (Jude 4).
7. Children who depart from the faith, by their actions, mark themselves (predispose themselves) for judgment (Jude 4).
8. Children who depart from the faith ignore the fact that, in their relationship with Christ, lip service is not life (Jude 5).
9. Children who depart from the faith experience the privileges associated with salvation, but, in rebellion that leads to judgment, they choose another way (Jude 6).
10. Children who depart from the faith are unrestrained in sin (Jude 7).
11. Children who depart from the faith know the truth, but rarely apply it (Jude 11).
12. Children who depart from the faith are nominally religious like Balaam, who knew enough of the truth to have a conversation about God but not enough of the truth to allow it to change his life (Jude 11).
13. Children who depart from the faith stand in the way of spiritual progress and truth (Jude 11).
14. Children who depart from the faith are concerned for self, not others (Jude 12).
15. Children who depart from the faith are all show, but little substance (Jude 12).
16. Children who depart from the faith show no evidence of salvation. (Jude 12).
17. Children who depart from the faith want to make a good impression and "keep up appearances," yet they live a double life (Jude 13).
18. Children who depart from the faith, without repentance, their path will never lead them any closer to a fulfilling (spiritually satisfying) relationship with Christ. (Jude 13).

19. To keep themselves from "turning aside" or from "turning away" from the faith, children should remember God's words (Jude 17).

20. To keep themselves from "turning aside" or from "turning away" from the faith, children can remain in God's way by practicing spiritual faithfulness (Jude 20–21).

21. To keep themselves from "turning aside" or from "turning away" from the faith, children can live outside of themselves by reaching out to others with the compassion of Jesus Christ (Jude 22–23).

22. There are reasons why God gave children parents (Proverbs 1:1–4).

23. Teach your children respect for authority in the home, and they will respect authority when they are outside the home (Proverbs 1:7–9).

24. Because peer groups can influence your child to engage in spiritually negative activities and live a life that does not please God, parents must monitor their child(ren)'s peer groups (Proverbs 1:10–16).

25. Concerning parental instruction, what children do with God's Word, when they are young, will determine the direction of their lives (Proverbs 2:1–5).

26. Because children need direction on their journey through life, children must trust God's guidebook: His Word (the Bible). (Proverbs 3:1–6).

27. Children must not waste the parental discipline they receive when they are young (Proverbs 3:11–12).

28. Often the bad decisions a child makes when he/she is young become stumbling blocks to the child's future success in life (Proverbs 3:21–26).

29. Just as parents have a responsibility to instruct their children in matters pertaining to biblical wisdom and godly understanding, children have a responsibility to both receive the parents' teachings when they are children and retain the parents' instruction for the rest of their lives (Proverbs 4:1–9).

30. A child's obedience adds to both the quality and quantity of the child's life (Proverbs 4:10–13, 20–23).

31. Be constantly vigilant concerning the "crowd" your child keeps and warn your child to flee immorality because immorality is sin (Proverbs 5:1–8, 20).

32. Manage your money wisely. (Proverbs 6:1–5, 20–23).

33. Just because a parent made mistakes when he/she was young does not mean that the child must make the same mistakes when he/she is young (Proverbs 7:1–3, 24–27).

34. Teach your children to keep their "spiritual commitments current" and to refuse to compromise with sin (Proverbs 8:1–4, 32).

35. Every child's work ethic is a self-portrait of his/her soul (Proverbs 10:1, 5).

36. Children must do more than humor their parents. Children must honor them (Proverbs 13:1, 14).

37. In being stronger than his/her child's strongest moments, the parent who loves his/her child disciplines, when needed (Proverbs 13:24).

38. God-honoring homes are a child's #1 place of refuge (Proverbs 14:26–27).

39. When children "get their way" when they are young, they will walk in "their own way" when they are older (Proverbs 15:20, 32).

40. The negative patterns children establish while they are young will come back to haunt them when they become adults (Proverbs 17:2).

41. Allow grandchildren to be the "joy" of grandparents (Proverbs 17:6).

42. Parents need to do everything they can to raise their children in such a way that the children do not "spoil" but instead leave behind a legacy that honors both God and the family's last name (Proverbs 17:21, 25, 28).

43. Parents must agree on a philosophy of discipline: Start early—be balanced—correct often (Proverbs 19:13, 18, 20, 25–27, 29).

44. Teach your children to live a life of integrity that is "character driven, not emotion led" (Proverbs 20:7).

45. A child who is swift to verbally disrespect his/her parent(s) reveals the condition of his/her heart (Proverbs 20:20–21).

46. When a child makes God the joy of His life, God rewards the child's faithfulness to Him (Proverbs 20:27, 29–30).

47. Because a child "bent" toward Christ will live his/her values when he/she is old, parents have a God-given responsibility to influence that child for the Lord (Proverbs 22:1, 6).

48. For your children, establish biblical boundaries, enforce them, and keep them in place (Proverbs 22:28, 23:10–11).

49. Be diligent in your discipline—your child's eternity may depend on it (Proverbs 23:13–14 with 22:15).

50. Obedient children cause their parents to be glad (Proverbs 23:22–28).

51. A child must not trust the influence of those who advise the child to "put aside" parental authority for authority outside the home (Proverbs 24:21–22).

52. Every parent with a disobedient child can feel Solomon's pain (Proverbs 27:11).

53. Since children are like lambs and need the nurturing of parents, lead them, feed them, and tend them as a shepherd tends his flock (Proverbs 27:23–24).

54. The stings of a child's unwise actions can leave permanent scars on the hearts of his/her parents (Proverbs 28:7).

55. In the life of a child, for every privilege there is an equal responsibility (Proverbs 28:24).

56. God will remove His blessing on children who, without repentance, harden their hearts toward Him (Proverbs 29:1–3).

57. In understanding that it is never too late to start parenting correctly, be a parent not a "(s) parent" (Proverbs 29:15, 17, 21).

58. Because God, not society, establishes a parent's guidelines for "all things children," be faithful to God and "stick by the stuff" (Proverbs 30:1, 11–15).

59. To prevent society's predators from successfully targeting your children, remain faithful in your responsibility to parent biblically (Proverbs 30:17).

60. Since children tend to repeat their unrepentant or unbelieving parents' mistakes, if you want your children to walk in the ways of the Lord—as a parent—you need to walk in God's ways yourself (Proverbs 31:1–3).

61. In a child's mind, there is nothing more precious than a godly mother (Proverbs 31:10, 28–29).

62. Whether prior to the Fall or after man's Fall in sin, God wants families to have children—biologically or through adoption (Genesis 1:28–29, 9:1).

63. You can be included in the fulfillment of God's promise to Abraham in Genesis 12:3 when you and your children form a salvation relationship with Christ (Genesis 12:1–3, Galatians 3:13–29).

64. One of God's commanded purposes for parents is that dad and mom would "keep (guard like a sentinel) the way of the Lord [and] do righteousness (practice biblically consistent right living) and [live justly before the Lord]" (Genesis 18:19).

65. Parenting requires sacrifice (Genesis 22:1–14, Hebrews 11:17–19).

66. Because God plays no favorites, neither should we—especially in the home (Genesis 37:1–2, 1 Samuel 16:1–15, Acts 10:34, Romans 2:11, Proverbs 28:21).

67. The worst that is offered by Christ is better than the best society has to offer (Exodus 2:1–10, Hebrews 11:10, 23–29).

68. The greatest blessing a child can have is godly parents (Exodus 20:1–5, Exodus 34:6–7; Numbers 14:18; Malachi 4:4–6).

69. Since, in the home, more is caught than taught, be a "priority" parent. Parent "incarnationally," by "living out" Jesus in what you do, where you go, what you say, and how you respond to life (Deuteronomy 6:4–9, 11:19; Psalm 128:1–4; Judges 2:10).

70. As your children get older, come to grips with the fact that, as you did when you were younger, they too will leave the home (Deuteronomy 32:11–12a; Genesis 2:24, 12:1–2; Matthew 19:5; John 3:16–17; Ephesians 5:31).

71. There is no greater joy in parenting than to know that your life's investment in your children's lives resulted in "service for the Savior" (Joshua 24:15, Isaiah 54:13, and 3 John 4).

72. The greatest calling any woman can have is motherhood (1 Samuel 1–2; Judges 13:2–5, 24–25; 2 Peter 1:8; Psalm 113:9; Jeremiah 1:5).

73. Since godly parents can have ungodly children, if parents "start early" and "stay balanced"— if parents discipline their children early, often, and in a balanced manner, and if believing parents do not neglect their children but instead enact "discipline that disciples," their children will be a blessing to them in old age (1 Samuel 2:12, 17; 2 Samuel 12:24, 14:28, 15:10; 2 Samuel 13 with 1 Kings 1–2; Proverbs 1:8–9, 13:24, 23:13–14, 29:15, 17; Luke 15:11–32; Hebrews 12:6).

74. God gave parents children to raise for the Lord, release back to God, and become sanctuaries for Jesus (Psalm 127:1–5, Psalm 139:13–16, and 128:1–4).

75. Since children are like "wet cement," just as a child left to himself/herself will be bent in the direction of the influence he/she receives from peer groups and society, a child bent toward Christ will practice biblical values when he/she is "old" (Proverbs 1:1–7, 3:1–6, 22:1–6; 1 Peter 2:2–3).

76. All lives are sacred, including the little "yet-to-be-born" lives in the womb waiting to be delivered. (Micah 6:7, Judges 11:30–40, Psalm 139:13–16, Jeremiah 1:5).

77. The parent's foremost responsibility is to lead his/her child to the Savior (Matthew 10:13–16, 18:2–6, 18:10, 19:14; Mark 9:36–37; Luke 17:1–2; 2 Timothy 1:5).

78. Right behavior and the child's biblically consistent response in the Lord is obedience to dad and mom as both father and mother parent together (Ephesians 6:1–4, Colossians 3:20, Proverbs 1:8–9).

79. It is the responsibility of both older and younger people to establish a pattern of godliness for other people to follow (1 Timothy 4:12–13; Titus 2:3–5, 6–8; Luke 2:40–52).

"Parenting by the Book"

(A Bible Study for Small Groups)

Study 1: History's First Family
(Genesis 4:1–7)

REREAD THE CONTENT IN GENESIS 4:1–7. From the following questions, discover and discuss some lessons from history's first family.

From Genesis 4:1–7:

1. Were Cain or Abel nurtured in vain?

2. Were Adam and Eve good parents—in society's eyes?

3. Were Adam and Eve good parents—in God's eyes?

4. Today, can children be nurtured in vain?

5. Choose one: is parenting a futile endeavor, a rewarding and fulfilling experience, or is it both (if in a group: discuss)?

6. In your opinion, did Adam and Eve name their second child based on the impressions and disappointments resulting from the raising of their first child, Cain?[116]

7. Knowing that every child of God is "accepted in the Beloved [One] (Jesus)" (see Ephesians 1:6), do all children have the potential to live a life that pleases God and fulfills His plan?

8. Living a life that reflects the child's love for Jesus, can every child overcome human expectations and live a life that God will bless?

9. If a family's first child does not live up to the parents' exalted expectations of being a doctor, a lawyer, or "someone successful in society," should parents expect the next child(ren) to exceed the expectations of the first?[117]

10. Of the two sons of history's first parents, which is remembered more: the one who expected God to honor the work of his hands or the son who trusted God to honor the worship of his heart (Abel still speaks: Hebrews 11:4)?

    If in a group, discuss the following lessons (from Genesis 4:1–7):

11. It is common for parents to expect great things from their children (Genesis 4:1).

12. God establishes the number of children each couple should have (Genesis 4:2, 5:3–5).

13. God wants His children to honor Him (Genesis 4:3–5a).

14. In your opinion, were Adam and Eve good parents (with Cain and Abel? Later, once Seth was born)?

Notes:

Study 2: Children Who Walk in "the Way of Cain"
2 Timothy 4:3–4; Jude

WHY DO CHILDREN WITH THE same parents and the same upbringing turn out so differently? Reread the content taken from 2 Timothy 4:3–4 and the book of Jude. Then, from the book of Jude, discover, answer, and discuss the following questions and statements on children who "turn away" and "turn aside" from God.

From Jude:

15. Define "the way of Cain" (see Jude 11; 2 Timothy 4:3–4; Hebrews 11:4; 1 John 3:12, 15).

16. See the author's content on 2 Timothy 4:3–4. In a matter that relates to child-rearing and the future lives of your children, define and discuss the following terms:

"Apostrophe" ("a turning away"):

Matthew 26:52

Matthew 27:3

Titus 1:14

Hebrews 12:25

Romans 11:26

Romans 12:19

"[Walking toward] Apostasy" ("a turning aside"):

1 Timothy 1:6

1 Samuel 2:30b

1 Timothy 6:20–21

17. From Jude 4–13, since many parents experience the heartache of having a child "turn away from" or "turn aside from" the truth, what characterizes children who defect, depart, disappear, leave, or fall away from their faith? How many of these characteristics are found in your child(ren)?

Characteristic: Found in my/our child(ren):

Jude 4   _____ Yes   _____ No

Jude 4   _____ Yes   _____ No

Jude 4   _____ Yes   _____ No

Jude 5   _____ Yes   _____ No

Jude 6   _____ Yes   _____ No

Jude 7   _____ Yes   _____ No

Jude 11   _____ Yes   _____ No

Jude 11   _____ Yes   _____ No

Jude 11   _____ Yes   _____ No

Jude 12   _____ Yes   _____ No

Jude 12   _____ Yes   _____ No

Jude 12   _____ Yes   _____ No

Jude 13   _____ Yes   _____ No

Jude 13   _____ Yes   _____ No

18. From Jude 17–23, what can children do to keep themselves from the apostrophe and/or apostasy of a relationship that has drifted away from Christ?

Jude 17

Jude 20–21

Jude 22–23

Notes:

Study 3: "Parenting by the Book" (1)
Ecclesiastes 1:2; Proverbs, Part 1

From Ecclesiastes 1:2:

Reread the content from Ecclesiastes 1:2 and Proverbs 1:1–4, 1:7–9, 1:10–16, 2:1–5, 3:1–6, 3:11–12, 3:21–26, 4:1–9, and 4:10–13, 20–23. Even though, in raising his son, Rehoboam, Solomon was something of a "failure" as a parent—knowing that Solomon's words in Proverbs were not his words but the inspired words of God, from the following passages, what lessons—on parenting—can you learn from Proverbs?

19. Is it possible, in part, that Solomon wrote the book of Ecclesiastes out of regret, in his own eyes, for being a failed national leader and, in God's eyes, for being a failure as a parent?

20. Could Solomon have been a more successful parent if he had invested more time in the life of his son (it was during Rehoboam's reign that the ten northern tribes rebelled against Solomon's son's leadership and divided the kingdom)?

From the book of Proverbs:

21. Yes or No: Are there Proverbs and other scripture passages that parents can apply when their children fail to live up to a parent's hopes or God's expectations? If so, make a list of the passages.

22. From Proverbs 1:2–4, list and discuss ten reasons why God gave children parents (list ten parental responsibilities, as given by God, and how you—as a parent—are fulfilling them).

23. In what ways can a parent teach his/her child to "take God seriously" and "fear the Lord" (see Proverbs 1:7–9)?

24. From Proverbs 1:10–16, since peer groups can influence your child to engage in spiritually negative activities and live a life that does not please God, what responsibilities do parents have concerning their child's peer groups (can a parent invite his/her child's peer groups over to the house for activities, meals, or other events or is parental engagement with a child's peer group "off limits")?

25. From Proverbs 2:1–5, Joshua 1:6–8), since God's estimation of success is based on the knowledge of God's Word and its application into life, what should parents counsel their children to do in order for their children to obtain the knowledge and wisdom that will help them live their lives in a manner that honors the Lord (review the three recommendations made in the study on Proverbs 2:1–5)?

26. Since a child who embraces parental discipline and God's Word is promised a longer life of increased quality, what should the child embrace and what can the child avoid in order to experience a longer life and a better quality of life (see Proverbs 3:1–6)?

27. From Proverbs 3:5–6, make a list of "your part" and make a separate list defining "God's part" in the "trust," "lean," and "acknowledge" aspects of relying on God for guidance.

    Discuss what it means to trust.

    Discuss what it means to lean.

    Discuss what it means to acknowledge.

28. What kind of an attitude adjustment is required in the life of a child if he/she appears to be "on the path" to "wasting" the parental discipline he/she receives as a child (see Proverbs 3:11–12)?

29. As it relates to Solomon's teachings in Proverbs 3:21–26, explain the "V" illustration (mentioned in the endnote) as it applies to the lifelong consequences of the "bad decisions" a person might make as a child.

30. As implied in Proverbs 4:1–9, when you were young what "bad" advice did your parents give you that you are not/will not give to your children and what "good" advice did your parents give you that you will pass down to your children?

31. How does a child's obedience add to the quality and quantity of a child's life (see Proverbs 4:10–13, 20–23)?

Notes:

Study 4: "Parenting by the Book" (2)
Proverbs, Part 2

Reread the content from Proverbs 5:1–8, 20; 6:1–5, 20; 7:1–3, 24–27; 8:1–4, 31–36; 10:1, 5; 13:1, 14; 13:24; 14:26–27; 15:20, 27; 17:2, 6. Even though, in raising his son, Rehoboam, Solomon was something of a "failure" as a parent—knowing that Solomon's words in Proverbs were not his words but the inspired words of God, from the following passages, what lessons—on parenting—can you learn from Proverbs?

32. In what ways does a child's immoral relationships—both physical and online—effect the future quality of a child's life (see Proverbs 5:1–8, 20; 1 Corinthians 15:33)?

33. What is the disadvantage of cosigning for a grown child's loan (see Proverbs 6:1–5, 20–23)?

34. In what ways can a parent warn his/her children to "not repeat" the mistakes the parent made when that parent was in his/her "growing up" years (see Proverbs 7:1–3, 24–27)?

35. What is the importance of a parent or a child keeping his/her "spiritual commitments current" (see Proverbs 8:1–4, 32)?

36. Since every child's work ethic is a self-portrait of his/her soul, discuss the truths Solomon shared concerning laziness, when found in a child (see Proverbs 10:1, 5; Proverbs 6:7, 9; 10:5, 26; 12:24–27; 13:4; 18:9; 19:15, 24; 20:4; 21:25–26; 22:13; 24:10).

    Proverbs 10:1, 5

    Proverbs 6:7

    Proverbs 6:9

    Proverbs 10:1, 5

Proverbs 10:26

Proverbs 12:24–27

Proverbs 13:4

Proverbs 18:9

Proverbs 19:15

Proverbs 19:24

Proverbs 20:4

Proverbs 21:25–26

Proverbs 22:13

Proverbs 24:10

37. How should a parent deal with his/her child when that child is a "scoffer" who merely humors his/her parent rather than a child who honors his/her parent in the Lord (see Proverbs 13:1, 14)?

38. As a parent, what is the value of, every time possible, being "stronger than" his/her child's "strongest moment" (see Proverbs 13:24)?

39. Describe ways that you, as a parent, can make your home a "safe place" for your child (see Proverbs 14:26–27)?

40. Discuss this principle: "When children "get their way" when they are young, they will walk in "their own way" when they are older" (see Proverbs 15:20, 32).

41. As implied in Proverbs 17:2, in what ways will the negative patterns children establish while they are young come back to haunt them when they become adults?

42. As a man with potentially hundreds of children, why did Solomon imply that his grandchildren were the "joy" of grandparents (see Proverbs 17:6)?

Notes:

Study 5: "Parenting by the Book" (3)
Proverbs, Part 3

Reread the content from Proverbs 17:21, 25, 28; 19:13, 18, 20, 25, 26–27, 29; 20:7, 20–21, 27, 29–30; 22:5–6, 28; 23:10–11. Even though, in raising his son, Rehoboam, Solomon was something of a "failure" as a parent—knowing that Solomon's words in Proverbs were not his words but the inspired words of God, from the following passages, what lessons—on parenting—can you learn from Proverbs?

43. Describe a "spoiled" child, the reasons the child is "spoiled," and what can be done to change the legacy an unrepentant "spoiled" child will leave behind (see Proverbs 17:21, 25, 28).

44. Since parents must "parent together," develop and define a "philosophy of parenting" of which both of you agree (see Proverbs 19:13, 18, 20, 25–27, 29).

45. What is the difference between your children living a life that is "character driven" rather than a life that is "emotion led" (see Proverbs 20:7)?

46. How should a parent deal with a child who "talks back to" his/her parent, and what are the consequences of a child who continues to disrespect his/her parents (see Proverbs 20:20–21)?

47. Make a list of the various ways that God will reward the life of a child who lives a life of faithfulness to God (see Proverbs 20:27, 29–30).

48. In detail, principle by principle, explain the truths presented in Proverbs 22:1, 6.

    In Proverbs 22:6, what does it mean to "train"?

    In Proverbs 22:6, what is a "child"?

In Proverbs 22:6, what is "the way"?

In Proverbs 22:6, define "old."

49. As implied in Proverbs 22:28 with Proverbs 23:10–11, define some boundaries that a parent should establish for his/her child—in the areas of behavior, morality, purity, companionships, friendships, and other vital areas of life.

Notes:

Study 6: "Parenting by the Book" (4)
Proverbs, Part 4

Reread the content from Proverbs 23:13–14 with 22:15; 23:22–28; 24:21–22; 27:11, 23–24; 28:7; 29:1–3, 15, 17, 21; 30:1, 11–15; 31:1–3, 10, 28–29. Even though, in raising his son, Rehoboam, Solomon was something of a "failure" as a parent—knowing that Solomon's words in Proverbs were not his words but the inspired words of God, from the following passages: what lessons—on parenting—can you learn from Proverbs?

50. In what ways does a child's biblical discipline benefit the child when he/she is older (see Proverbs 23:13–14 with 22:15)?

51. Emotionally and in other ways, what is the parental response to a child who obeys as compared to when a child disobeys (see Proverbs 23:22–28)?

52. Other than the voice/influence of the parent, what other voices—in society—vie for your child's attention (see Proverbs 24:21–22)?

53. Knowing of Solomon's lack of success in raising his son, Rehoboam, describe Solomon's parental pain (see Proverbs 27:11).

54. In what ways are children like lambs who need to be shepherded (see Proverbs 27:23–24)?

55. Discuss the following statement: The stings of a child's unwise actions can leave permanent scars on the hearts of his/her parents (Proverbs 28:7).

56. How can a parent "build trust" with his/her child (see Proverbs 28:24)?

57. When a child "hardens" his/her neck (heart) to a parent's discipline, what blessings will God remove from that child's life (see Proverbs 29:1–3)?

58. In understanding that it is never too late to start parenting correctly, are you a parent or a "(s) parent" (see Proverbs 29:15, 17, 21)?

59. In your family, who or what establishes the guidelines for raising your children—God or society (see Proverbs 30:1, 11–15)?

60. As a parent, what safeguards do you establish, in your home, to prevent society's predators from targeting your children (see Proverbs 30:17)?

61. Since, if you want your children to walk in the ways of the Lord,—as a parent—you need to walk in God's ways yourself, what intentional actions do you take to model Christianity in your home (see Proverbs 31:1–3)?

62. From Proverbs 31:10–31, define the role of a godly mother (establish a list of qualities that characterize a virtuous woman).

    Proverbs 31:10, 12

    Proverbs 31:11–12

    Proverbs 31:13–15

Proverbs 31:16–20

Proverbs 31:21–25

Proverbs 31:26–31

Notes:

Study 7: Principles for Parenting (1)
Selected Scriptures 1

Reread the content in the section entitled "How to Raise an Abel When the World is Raising Cain" from the Genesis 1:28–29 entry through the Deuteronomy 6:4–9 entry. Look up the references, read the passages, and discuss the following truths:

1. Whether prior to the Fall or after man's Fall into sin, God wants families to have children— biologically or through adoption (Genesis 1:28–29, 9:1).

2. You can be included in the fulfillment of God's promise to Abraham in Genesis 12:3 when you and your children form a salvation relationship with Christ (Genesis 12:1–3, Galatians 3:13–29).

3. One of God's commanded purposes for parents is that dad and mom would "keep (guard like a sentinel) the way of the Lord [and] do righteousness (practice biblically consistent right living) and [live justly before the Lord]" (Genesis 18:19).

4. Parenting requires sacrifice (Genesis 22:1–14 with Hebrews 11:17–19).

5. Because God plays no favorites, neither should we—especially in the home (Genesis 37:1–2, 1 Samuel 16:1–15, Acts 10:34, Romans 2:11, Proverbs 28:21).

6. Because God plays no favorites, neither should we—especially in the home (Acts 10:34, Romans 2:11, Proverbs 28:21).

7. The worst that is offered by Christ is better than the best society has to offer (Exodus 2:1–10; Hebrews 11:10, 23–29).

8. The greatest blessing a child can have is godly parents (Exodus 20:1–5, 34:6–7; Numbers 14:18; Malachi 4:4–6).

9. Since, in the home, more is caught than taught, be a "priority" parent. Parent "incarnationally," by "living out" Jesus in what you do, where you go, what you say, and how you respond to life (Deuteronomy 6:4–9, 11:19; Psalm 128:1–4; Judges 2:10).

10. As your children get older, come to grips with the fact that, as you did when you were younger, they too will leave the home (Deuteronomy 32:11–12a, Genesis 2:24, 12:1–2; Matthew 19:5; John 3:16–17; Ephesians 5:31).

Notes:

Study 8: Principles for Parenting (2)
Selected Scriptures 2

Reread the content in the section entitled "How to Raise an Abel When the World is Raising Cain. From the Joshua 24:15 entry through the 1 Timothy 4:12–13 entry, look up the references, read the passages, and discuss the following truths:

11. There is no greater joy in parenting than to know that your life's investment in your children's lives resulted in "service for the Savior" (Joshua 24:15, Isaiah 54:13, and 3 John 4).

12. The greatest calling any woman can have is motherhood (1 Samuel 1–2; Judges 13:2–5, 24–25; 2 Peter 1:8; Psalm 113:9; Jeremiah 1:5).

13. Since godly parents can have ungodly children, if parents "start early" and "stay balanced"—if parents discipline their children early, often, and in a balanced manner and if believing parents do not neglect their children but instead enact "discipline that disciples," their children will be a blessing to them in old age (1 Samuel 2:12, 17; 2 Samuel 12:24, 14:28, 15:10; 2 Samuel 13 with 1 Kings 1–2; Proverbs 1:8–9, 13:24, 23:13–14, 29:15, 17; Luke 15:11–32; Hebrews 12:6).

14. God gave parents children to raise for the Lord, release back to God, and become sanctuaries for Jesus (Psalm 127:1–5, 139:13–16, 128:1–4).

15. Since children are like "wet cement," just as a child left to himself/herself will be bent in the direction of the influence he/she receives from his/her peer groups and society, a child bent toward Christ will practice biblical values when he/she is "old" (Proverbs 1:1–7, 3:1–6, 22:1–6; 1 Peter 2:2–3).

16. All lives are sacred, including the little "yet-to-be-born" lives in the womb waiting to be delivered. (Micah 6:7, Judges 11:30–40, Psalm 139:13–16, Jeremiah 1:5).

17. The parent's foremost responsibility is to lead his/her child to the Savior (Matthew 10:13–16; 18:2–6, 10; 19:14; Mark 9:36–37; Luke 17:1–2; 2 Timothy 1:5).

18. Right behavior and the child's biblically consistent response to/in the Lord is obedience to dad and mom as both father and mother parent together (Ephesians 6:1–4, Colossians 3:20, Proverbs 1:8–9).

19. It is the responsibility of both older and younger people to establish a pattern of godliness for other people to follow (1 Timothy 4:12–13; Titus 2:3–5, 6–8; Luke 2:40–52).

Notes:

Study 9: Principles for Parenting (3)
Selected Scriptures 3

Read the "Family Favorites" section of the book *How to Raise an Abel When the World Is Raising Cain*, make any comments that God brings to your mind, and then, by way of review, answer and discuss the following questions from the Genesis 1:28–29 entry through the 1 Timothy 4:12–13 entry.

1. In modern times—biologically or through adoption—how can believing parents fulfill God's command to Adam and Eve to "be fruitful and multiply" (Genesis 1:28–29, 9:1)?

2. From Genesis 12:1–3 with Galatians 3:13–29, how can you, as a parent, be part of the fulfillment of God's promise to Abraham that through Abraham's "spiritual offspring" "all the families of the earth shall be blessed" (see Genesis 12:3)?

3. Why did God give children parents (Genesis 18:19)?

4. What sacrifices does parenting require—physically, spiritually, mentally, vocationally, geographically, financially, psychologically, emotionally, and in other ways (Genesis 22:1–14, Hebrews 11:17–19)?

Physically:

Spiritually:

Mentally:

Vocationally:

Geographically:

Financially:

Psychologically:

Emotionally:

In other ways:

5. What are the advantages and/or disadvantages of showing favoritism to one or more of your children. Is it ever appropriate to favor one child over another (Genesis 37:1–2, 1 Samuel 16:1–15, Acts 10:34, Romans 2:11, Proverbs 28:21)?

    Advantages:

    Disadvantages:

    _____Yes _____No _____Favoritism? It all depends!

6. Knowing that children become adults, do parents have an obligation to raise their children with a view of how God will use them in the future (Exodus 2:1–10; Hebrews 11:10, 23–29)?

7. Since the greatest blessing a child can have is to have godly parents and since, in the home, "more is caught than taught," in what ways are you, as a parent, "working on" being a more godly parent—in private and in public (Exodus 20:1–5, 34:6–7; Numbers 14:18; Malachi 4:4–6)?

8. As a parent, how obvious is your Christianity? Other than the times you talk about Jesus, can your children see Jesus in you in the morning when you get up, as you drive your child to school, in the evenings when everyone is home, and on the weekends when everyone is "merely being themselves" (Deuteronomy 6:4–9, 11:19; Psalm 128:1–4; Judges 2:10)?

9. Describe the emotions of both the parents and their children when the children "leave the nest" (see Deuteronomy 32:11–12a; Genesis 2:24, 12:1–2; Matthew 19:5; John 3:16–17; Ephesians 5:3).

10. Since your children will, more than likely, become "you" one day, what do they see in you today that they should be like and that they should not be like (Joshua 24:15, Isaiah 54:13, 3 John 4)?

11. Since having children is rarely about the parent and always about God—beyond prayer—what must each parent do for their children (1 Samuel 1–2; Judges 13:2–5, 24–25; 2 Peter 1:8; Psalm 113:9; Jeremiah 1:5)?

12. Since even godly parents can have ungodly children, what must you do, as a parent, to help your child change the spiritual direction of his/her life? Are you a parent or a "(s)parent" (1 Samuel 2:12, 17 with 2 Samuel 12:24, 14:28, 15:10; 2 Samuel 13 with 1 Kings 1–2; Proverbs 1:8–9, 13:24, 23:13–14, 29:15, 17; Luke 15:11–32; Hebrews 12:6)?

Changes:

_____Parent _____(S)parent _____I am a little of both—sometimes a parent, other times a "(s)parent"

13. In the context of raising your child for the Lord and, picturing child-raising as an archer with a bow (see Psalm 127:4), describe ways that you child should be "shot" (Psalm 127:1–5, 139:13–16, and 128:1–4).

The bowstring of correction is loose:

The bowstring of correction is too tight:

The bowstring of correction is "just right":

14. In what ways are children like "wet cement" (Proverbs 1:1–7, 3:1–6, 22:1–6; 1 Peter 2:2–3)?

15. On which of society's altars do modern-day parents sacrifice their children? In how many ways do believing parents do the same (Micah 6:7, Judges 11:30–40, Psalm 139:13–16, Jeremiah 1:5)?

16. What are the primary roles of a parent as each seeks to develop his/her child physically, spiritually, mentally, vocationally, geographically, financially, psychologically, emotionally, and in other ways (Matthew 10:13–16, 18:2–6, 10, and 19:14; Mark 9:36–37; Luke 17:1–2; 2 Timothy 1:5)?

Physically:

Spiritually:

Mentally:

Vocationally:

Geographically:

Financially:

Psychologically:

Emotionally:

In other ways:

17. How does the child benefit by responding with proper obedience, by showing sincere respect, and by placing a high value (honor) on dad and mom, in the home (Ephesians 6:1–4, Colossians 3:20, Proverbs 1:8–9)?

In quality of life:

In quantity of life:

18. Make a list of the ways a child or teenager can be a spiritual example to others (see 1 Timothy 4:12–13, Luke 2:40–52).

    1 Timothy 4:12–13:

    Luke 2:40–52:

    (For older adults, see also Titus 2:3–5, 6–8.)

Notes:

Principles for Parenting

See your child not as he is but as he could be.

Be a priority parent not a perfect one.

Your child's most important teacher is not in his classroom. It's you.

Never parent alone. Added support results in added value. Seek help, when needed.

Do everything possible to influence the influencers of your children.

Never wait for the church to grow your child spiritually. Start the process at home.

Who you are makes all the difference in the progress of your child, so trust God first, last, and always.

Anyone can be a father, but it takes a special person to be a dad.

If you want your children to find a Father in God, there needs to be something of God in their father.

Since parents have a profound effect on the future of their children, be careful how you parent (see Numbers 14:18).

Since nations are built child by child, the welfare and future of all mankind rests on the shoulders of parents (see Malachi 4:6).

Pointers for parents: discipline (selected scripture).

1. Be balanced in your approach (Proverbs 29:15, 17).
2. Be biblical in your approach. (Proverbs 6:23).
3. Be actively involved in the privilege of parenting (Proverbs 22:1, 6).
4. Start early (Proverbs 13.24).
5. Stay balanced (Proverbs 22:15).
6. Be consistent (Proverbs 22:5).

Notes:

SALVATION!

IT'S FREE!

---

4. **ASK JESUS INTO YOUR LIFE**
   But as many as received Jesus,
   to them God gave the power (ability)
   to become the children of God—
   to as many as trust in His name.
   (John 1:12)

   Receive Jesus into your life right now!

   Prayer:
   Dear God, I admit I am a sinner. I deserve pun-
   ishment. Jesus took my place. I pray to receive
   Jesus Christ today. I ask Jesus into my life to
   forgive me of my sins. In Jesus' name I pray.
   Amen.

   ASSURANCE: 1 John 5:11-13

   Name: _____

   Date: _____

WHAT MUST I DO TO BE SAVED?

1. **ADMIT: YOU ARE A SINNER**
   For all have sinned and come short
   of the glory of God.
   (Romans 3:23)

   The glory of God is the standard you must
   meet to enter God's heaven.

   ALL HAVE SINNED—YOU HAVE SINNED.

2. **ACKNOWLEDGE: SIN DESERVES**
   PUNISHMENT
   For the wages of sin is death...
   (Romans 6:23a)

   Wages are what you earn.
   Death is separation.
   The result of sin is separation from God—
   forever.

   ALL DESERVE PUNISHMENT—
   YOU DESERVE PUNISHMENT.

---

3. **ACKNOWLEDGE: JESUS TOOK**
   AND EXPERIENCED YOUR
   PUNISHMENT FOR YOU
   But God demonstrated His love toward us,
   in that while we were yet sinners,
   Christ died for us.
   (Romans 5:8)

   JESUS DIED FOR SINNERS—
   JESUS DIED FOR YOU.

   Because of Jesus Christ, you do not
   have to be punished!

   WHAT MUST I DO TO BE SAVED?

Bibliography

Bible. New King James Version. Nashville, TN: Thomas Nelson, 1982.

Campbell, Ross. "A Careful Man I Want to Be." *How to Really Love Your Child*. Wheaton, IL: Victor Books, 1977.

MacArthur, Douglas. "Build Me a Son." Source unknown.

Marshall, Catherine. "The Keeper of the Spring." *Mr. Jones, Meet the Master*. New York: Fleming H. Revell, 1951, 147–48.

Pisani, Keith D. *Jesus Loves Me: A Follow-Up Guide for Children*. Bloomington, IN: Westbow Press, 2017.

_____. "Salvation: It's Free" Gospel Tract.

_____. *Spiritual Lessons for Growing Believers*. (Bloomington, IN: Westbow Press, 2016.

Swindoll, Charles R. "Someday." *Man to Man*. Grand Rapids: MI, Zondervan, 1996, 360–361.

_____. "Twelve Rules for Raising Delinquent Children." *You and Your Child*. Insight for Living, 1998, 63–64.

Endnotes

1 All scripture quotations are taken from the 1982 New King James Version of the Bible, unless otherwise noted.

2 In reading the "Parenting by the Book/Principles from Proverbs" section, it would be good for parents to study each Proverbs entry—one passage at a time—and, each time you meet with your children for devotions, read one "section entry" each time, with discussion and prayer.

3 When reading this manual on child-raising, it is a good idea to read the endnotes! Since the endnotes give content in addition to what is found in the main body of the manual, perhaps the best way to benefit from the "added content" found in the endnotes is as follows: (1) read the entire content on the page that you are currently reading and then read the endnotes at the end of the manual, or (2) read each endnote as it occurs, placing your finger on the manual's "main text"—as you read the endnote—so you will not lose your place. Either way, thank you for reading this endnote. Hopefully, the reading of it will help.

4 This is the author's impression of what that first "family moment" had to be like.

5 Because both sons were sinners, conception had to take place *after* Adam's Fall into sin. Otherwise, Cain and Abel would have been born sinless.

6 Some would interpret the Hebrew word *qayin* (Cain) as meaning "possession of God" having been conceived with the "help of God." In recognizing the role of God in her son's conception, by the time of Cain's birth Eve evidenced enough faith in God to trust God for offspring.

7 Not knowing what took place in the pre-creation counsels of God concerning the Fall of man, could this "alternate scenario" have played out. Between the moment that Eve ate "of the fruit" of the tree of the knowledge of good and evil and prior to the next moment that Adam "took of the fruit" and ate with her, thus plunging mankind into sin (Romans 5:12, 19 clearly teaches that man's Fall was because of Adam, not Eve), was it possible for God—in that moment between Eve's action and Adam's sin—to both remove and replace Eve with another woman who had not yet eaten of the fruit and who would not have eaten of the fruit—ever—thus eliminating Adam's temptation to eat of the fruit? Would this have changed history and eliminated the curses associated with the Fall—including a mother's "pain in childbirth?" Because "death" was a part of the curse also, most would say no because there would be no "removing and replacing Eve"—through death—prior to the Fall (biblically, contrary to the teachings of evolution, there was no death prior to the Fall). As a result, the consequences of the Fall remain on Adam who, as the head of his home and the head of the race, chose to disobey God and sin. Thankfully, Christ did not have a "biological" father to pass down

sin to Him. Conceived of the Holy Spirit, Jesus was born sinless and was thus "fully qualified" to be our only all-sufficient sacrifice for sin (see 2 Corinthians 5:21).

8   It would not be difficult to speculate that an abortion of Abel would have played into Satan's purposes to prevent God's promised Deliverer from being born or from "bruising/crushing" Satan's head (see Genesis 3:15). But even the death of Abel later, by the hand of Cain, did not stop God from bringing forth the One (Jesus) Who would "save His people from their sins" (Matthew 1:21).

9   Perhaps, in sacrificing the blood of an approved animal, Abel learned from Adam and Eve's failed attempt to cover themselves with fig leaves grown in ground that God had cursed (Genesis 3:7). Perhaps Abel recognized that it took the shedding of the blood of an animal for God to clothe Adam and Eve with coats of skin (Genesis 3:21—perhaps Adam and Eve told their sons of their "mistake"). As a result, was it Abel's discernment that resulted in Abel offering the shed blood of an animal to God? Was it a lack of discernment that resulted in Cain offering the works of Cain's hands (his "fig leaves") to God? In offering the "fruit of the ground" to God, did Cain do so because his parents—in covering themselves with fig leaves—had attempted that method of "covering" their sin first? Parents are not perfect. Although, in the home, children will do what parents do more than what parents say, children do need to learn from their parents' mistakes.

10 See Hebrews 11 for a list and description of others whom God inducted into His Hall of Faith.

11 Was Judas saved or lost? This is a question commonly asked of children who turn away from the Bible's teachings. Although not all children who "turn away" should be compared to Judas, in Acts 1:16–20, 25, when Judas's rope broke (see Matthew 27:3–10) and he went to "his own place," the body of Judas fell into Jerusalem's Hinnom Valley, which is transliterated into the Greek as the "Valley of-Gehenna" which is the ravine outside of Jerusalem that served as the garbage dump for the city. Since it was a location that burned with fire twenty-four hours a day, 365 days a year (360 days in a Jewish year), in the minds of the locals, Gehenna pictured hell. If one picture is worth a thousand words, then, when Judas went to "his own place," he went to a place that burned with a never-ending fire. The author would argue that Judas was lost. If that is the case, then, wishful thinking aside, are children who apostatize also lost spiritually? If so, then parents must do everything they can to provide spiritual intervention for their children who "turn away from" God's truths.

12 In Samuel 2:30b, the Hebrew term *despise* is the equivalent to the English word *contempt*.

13 The author, Keith D. Pisani, has written a children's follow-up guide that facilitates the spiritual growth of a new convert in Christ. Published by Westbow Press, it is *Jesus Loves Me: A Follow-Up Guide for Children*.

14 In Genesis 13:12, Lot pitched his tent toward Sodom. In Genesis 13:18, Abram "removed" his tent from any view of Sodom and put distance between himself and evil. As God's children, it is important for us to walk so closely with God that the devil cannot squeeze in between.

15 If, from the original Greek, the alternate translation of "spots in your feasts of charity" is accepted ("hidden rocks" in a harbor), then children whose hearts are not right with God are like reefs in the water that can rise at any moment to strike, shipwreck, or break up a family that so desperately wants to honor the Lord. Make sure your family steers clear of the rocks. It only takes one "bad apple" to ruin the bushel. Be constantly aware of the intents of your child's heart. Maintain a unity in the home that is centered on God and His Word.

16 These questions are repeated in the "Parenting by the Book" Small Group Bible Section found later in this manual on parenting.

17 Were Cain and Abel twins, or was Abel born after Cain was weaned?

18   While acknowledging God's commandment to "be fruitful and multiply," this question is in light of Eve's potential frustration with her first son, Cain, which may have resulted in the conception and birth of Eve's second son, Abel.

19   Three thousand and twenty-six years is calculated from 4003 BC (the time of Cain and Abel) to 977 BC (the accepted date of the writing of Ecclesiastes).

20   See 1 Kings 11:1–3.

21   With so many wives, concubines, and lovers, it is possible that Solomon had hundreds, if not thousands, of children.

22   See 1 Kings 3:5–15 and 1 Chronicles 1:7–12.

23   Consider this: since most of Solomon's wives, concubines, and lovers were the means by which foreign kings and powers "guaranteed treaties" and other diplomatic relationships with Solomon, how many of these wives, concubines, and lovers worshiped the God of the Bible and shared Solomon's values? In their tents, on Jerusalem's "Embassy Row," most of these wives, concubines, and lovers had idol shelves, worshiped false gods, and were left by Solomon to raise their mutual offspring according to the values of prevailing society— according to the wisdom of their world. "Society's values" is a wisdom that compromises biblical child-rearing principles in Christian homes today.

24   In addition, could Ecclesiastes be Solomon's subtle lament over one of his own "lost sons," as was Abel, who was "lost" to Adam and Eve when Cain killed Abel (knowing the sad state of his children's upbringing provided by their idol-worshiping moms—in all probability—Solomon's son would have been "lost" spiritually while Abel was "lost" to Adam and Eve physically, in death)?

25   This is not an exhaustive list.

26   In the current church age, the biblical perspective is to live a "Christ-honoring" life.

27   Never forget that most of scripture was written in "terms of personalities." As a result, discover a biblical personality that resembles or most resembles your child and make appropriate applications as you parent your child.

28   Since, within seven years of graduation from high school, a child selects his/her college, vocation (career), location, "his/her own" commitment to Christ, and mate, can the parent still provide influence and insights concerning these decisions even after the child is out of the house? Absolutely, yes! Just because a child leaves the nest, are you still a parent? Yes. Your "parent card" never expires—even after death (see Hebrews 11:4—"Though dead, Abel yet speaks"). Be careful of the values promoted by your child's "college of choice." Since you raised your child to honor God for a lifetime, refuse to allow some "God-denying/evolution-entrenched" professor in a secular institution—who embraces society's values—to influence your child to deny his/her faith (see the 2 Timothy 4:3–4 study on the terms "apostrophe" and "apostasy," which define a life that "turns aside" or "turns away from" God's truths to follow man's errors). In every chosen vocation, your children can honor God.

29   Since the Bible is seen as a door through which the child can walk to get to life, by studying the Psalms, a child can learn discretion as he/she identifies with the circumstances of the life of David, who was known as a "man after God's own heart" (see Acts 13:22), primarily because David always repented of his sin(s).

30   Solomon repeated this truth in Proverbs 9:10 when he added that "the fear of the Lord is the beginning of (another necessary ingredient for) wisdom" (Proverbs 9:10).

31   In Proverbs, four types of fools were revealed. Since Solomon's son, Rehoboam, was a fool on four different levels, notice the chronological sequence of a child's foolish belief and unwise behavior. First level: The "simpleton" devoid of understanding who turns away from wisdom (see Proverbs 1:22; 7:7; 9:4, 16; 14:15; 1:32;

14:18, 24). Second level: The "scoffer" who laughs at wisdom, toys with wickedness, and rejects instruction (see Proverbs 1:22; 3:34; 9:7–8; 13:1; 14:6; 15:12; 19:29; 21:24; 22:10; 24:9). Third level: The "arrogant" person consumed by self-willed pride (see Proverbs 1:22; 1:32; 12:23; 13:16; 14:16; 15:20; 17:12; 18:2; 19:29; 23:9; 26:3). Fourth level: The "rebel" who so hates God's wisdom that he/she becomes an aggressive unbeliever who turns away from God's truth (see Proverbs 1:7; 10:8, 10; 10:21; 12:15; 14:9; 15:5; 16:22; 20:3; 27:22). In other words, parents can know if they have raised a fool and, at what level of foolishness the child exists, when their child cannot tell the difference between what is good and what is evil (the simpleton), laughs at wisdom derived from scripture or from godly parents (the scoffer), lives with one philosophy: "What's in it for me? Is this to my advantage?" (the arrogant), and, as an aggressive unbeliever who casts aside all that God embraces, rebels against authority, and lacks submission to the precepts and principles given by God (the rebel). Is your child wise or otherwise? The difference is respect for God and for His authorities in the home (see James 3:13–18). In adding one historical note: upon Solomon's death—by popular demand—Solomon's servant Jeroboam ruled the ten northern tribes of Israel (only Judah and Benjamin followed Rehoboam). Disrespectful as a son, King Rehoboam's people disrespected him. Having a crown on his head, Rehoboam had no chains of honor around his neck. It all started in the home.

32   In addition, the husband "who does not respect his wife" rarely receives respect from his children. Often the husband who does not function as the head of his home receives less respect from his children. Headship should not be a hardship for the husband, the wife, or the children.

33   From Proverbs 1:8, a primary role of the father is to teach and model respect for authority while the primary role of the mother is to teach the child(ren) the scriptures. Obviously, these roles can overlap, especially in a one-parent home.

34   The triune godhead had a "let us" also in Genesis 11:7. The godhead's "let us" always carries more authority than man's.

35   Since most Westerners seem to be "visual," here is an exercise in visualization: visualize a "laid-out [picnic] blanket," which pictures your child's heart or mind. With what—from God's Word or from your personal knowledge and experiences—can you fill this blanket?

36   Children who honor their parents obey their parents, in the Lord (see Ephesians 6:1–4 and Colossians 3:20). In scripture, obedience seems to be a "love" response by children to their parents. To the level that a child truly loves his dad or mom, the child will obey.

37   In redeeming His time in your life, God will "pack more" into your life.

38   The term *mercy* is the Hebrew term *chesed*, which is God's "covenant loyalty." It is the fact that God keeps His Word. In studying the Old Testament scriptures, when you see the word *mercies*, think of the word *loving-kindness* and appreciate the fact that what God promises, He performs (for examples of passages where the term *chesed* appears, see Genesis 39:21, Numbers 14:18–19, Jeremiah 31:3, Psalm 26:3, Lamentations 3:22–24, and, as mentioned in 1 Peter 1:3, because of God's abundant and overflowing loving-kindness, God has "birthed" us again spiritually to an ever-present reality of hope through the resurrection of Jesus Christ from the dead). Praise God that He keeps His Word to us.

39   Upon examining the experience of many children, when a child arrives at the age when he/she leaves home, how often does the now-grown child "leave behind" both the home and the values the child's parents taught him/her? If the now-grown child does "leave behind" the biblical values of the parents, are these scenarios possible: (1) the parent(s) did not adequately teach God's values in the home, or, (2) The child did not commit himself/herself to those biblical values, or, (3) A little of both (#1 and #2).

40 Because, often, a child is known by the crowd that he/she keeps, one of the best ways to keep God's Word before your child's eyes is to make sure that your child selects believing friends who live lives that please Jesus (the influence of peer groups can be positive as well as negative). Because "bad company corrupts good morals" (see 1 Corinthians 15:33), associating with godly friends is a benefit that, often, includes a "mutual accountability factor" among those friends and leads to spiritual growth in the life of your child.

41 For further study in Proverbs 3:5–6, when examining each line of the text (from "comma to comma"), determine "God's part" in each recommendation and "our part"—the individual's biblical/life response—to each command given by God.

42 It is through prayer that God overcomes principalities and powers, takes down Satan's strongholds, and frees your children from sin's chains and society's influences that put a stranglehold on your children's lives. Therefore, "pray without ceasing" by being in a "continual attitude of prayer" (see 1 Thessalonians 5:17). Heaven's power is in every prayer a parent prays.

43 I've often used the "V" illustration when discussing current decisions that impact the future direction of life. Draw a "V." The intersection of the "V's" two sides (at the bottom of the "V") pictures the time in life when a decision is made. Without God's intervention, from the time that decision is made, every future circumstance is within the outside lines of that "V." Initially the space between those lines is limited to the child's immediate geographical/environmental surroundings. But, as the outside lines are extended through time or circumstances, the space between those lines encompasses "much more vast" areas of life. Initially, if the decision (whether good or bad) is made in a room, the area between the lines is limited to that room. But extended beyond the room—beyond the windows, the walls, and the doors—that decision impacts every experience of life. Extended out, the dimension of both good and bad decisions encompasses the circumference of the world and eternity beyond. Be involved in your children's decisions. Without intervention or repentance, bad decisions today will negatively impact what is found in the future circumference of your child's life.

44 Being the son of David was something of a two-edged sword. Solomon was identified as the son of a king *and* the son of a father. As the son of a king, when David did something well the "good feelings" trickled down to Solomon. When David sinned or lost a battle, did the nation's "bad feelings" also trickle down to Solomon (during Solomon's "growing up" years)? Often children are known by the successes or failures of their parents. If that is the case, when do children develop their own identities?

45 Even "wayward" children, when they "come home" for a holiday, find it awkward to offend the values of the dad or mom who raised them.

46 What goes around comes around! Often the respect we show to others will be the respect that others return to us.

47 For parents, Solomon listed "passing on" instruction—which leads to wisdom—as one of the ten reasons God gave children parents (see Proverbs 1:2).

48 In his book *Improving Your Serve* (Chuck Swindoll, *Improving Your Serve* (Nashville: Thomas A. Nelson, 2004)) on pages 99–100, author Chuck Swindoll quoted Catherine Marshall from her book *Mr. Jones, Meet the Master* (New York: Fleming H. Revell, 1951) on pages 147–48 when she shared her husband Peter Marshall's story of "The Keeper of the Spring," who was charged with making sure that an Austrian town's spring was free of any debris that might clog the waterway and keep fresh water from flowing into the lake below. One day, the city council met, and, due to budget cuts, decided to "lay off" the keeper of the spring. Soon, the spring became clogged with leaves and branches. The water ceased to flow. Townspeople became sick. As believers, we must keep "the spring of our heart" clean so that the words and lessons we learned, as children, from our parents will continue to flow in all their purity throughout our entire lives. "Keep your

heart with all diligence (custody and awareness), for out of [that spring] are the issues [that matter] in life" (Proverbs 4:23).

49 From his experiences with his many concubines and wives, Solomon knew that the decision to commit adultery is (often) "sealed with a kiss." Solomon added that "a flattering tongue," a woman's "beauty," and her "alluring eyelids" can be factors, as well (see Proverbs 6:24–25).

50 As difficult as it sounds, just because you "know" the person or that a person is "family" does not mean that the person automatically is eligible for a loan or for the cosigning of a loan. Proverbs prohibits cosigning, which—for all practical purposes—is the granting of a loan. If you do grant a "non-cosigned" loan, make sure the person passes all the requirements of responsibility that a "non-relative/non-acquaintance/non-friend" would need to pass in order to get the loan. Since the receiving of a loan carries with it both a privilege (receiving the loan) and a responsibility (paying back the debt associated with the loan), consider both aspects of privilege and responsibility before granting any loan.

51 Because God is the Father of the saved, every believer has more than one father. If the earthly father is immoral or succumbed to other categories of temptation, recognize that your heavenly Father is pure and never sinned. In relation to every relationship known to God or man, the believer's heavenly Father stated, "You be holy, for I am holy, [says the Lord]" (1 Peter 1:16). Make the choice to walk in the footsteps of your heavenly Father. As you keep yourself pure, be reminded that immorality is merely one entry on the list of many additional temptations and sins in which a child's parent(s) may have been involved. As a parent—especially if you are a parent who has "been there" and "done that"—you can anticipate the temptations as you watch your child grow. As a result, continually guard your child's heart, sight, and consideration of the other sins on the list that you—as the parent—committed or could have committed when you were young. Also recognize this: every generation has "new" ways to commit "old" sins. Be aware. Anticipate. Intervene often—even if your intervention is "preemptive" rather than "reactive." Then answer this question: must you admit your "growing up" sins to your child? No! The Bible teaches that you must admit/confess your sins to God (1 John 1:9). Once you do, allow those sins to be covered by the blood of Christ at the foot of His cross.

52 Rehoboam's father, Solomon, had seven hundred wives, three hundred concubines, and many other [international] lovers. How did Solomon acquire so many? Did all of them merely "jump into his lap," or did he have to pursue them? Like father, like son? Solomon invested much instruction time in telling his son to "do what Solomon says and not do what Solomon does." Because a son is never required, by God, to walk in the footsteps of a sinning father, the sins of the father must not be reproduced in the life of his son.

53 Of Solomon's seven hundred wives, three hundred concubines, and many other [international] lovers, not one was his sister. When God inspired His Word, He was specific. Even society frowns on sexual relationships with a person's sister (if Solomon did have a relationship with his sister, he would have lost his kingdom). Knowing this, God defined "wisdom" as the one woman with whom both Solomon and Rehoboam could not commit adultery, without consequence. Knowing that, of all siblings, sisters are unafraid to "get in your face, share an opinion, and tell you what's what," form a close and pure relationship with spiritual "wisdom" and, as your closest kin, "she" will both warn you and keep you from sexual sins.

54 On a cold winter's night, as a boy, the future pathfinder of Africa and missionary pioneer David Livingstone attended a church service. Working the pump organ—other than the speaker—Livingstone was the only male there. When the speaker (missionary Robert Moffat) quoted Proverbs 8:4, "To you, O men, I call. My voice is to the sons of men," Livingstone believed that the passage was speaking directly to him. In response, he obeyed God's call to the missions. The rest is modern Christian history. In addition, Livingstone's call was

so clear that, when he died, although his body was buried at Westminster Abbey in London (England), his heart remained in Africa.

55 By way of review, from Proverbs 1:2, "wisdom" is uncommon sense in an uncommon degree (1 Kings 3:16–28), biblical discernment (Matthew 16:3), the ability to make choices approved by God (Proverbs 5:1), and "the God-given ability to make God-informed and God-centered decisions in life" (James 1:5–6).

56 By way of review, from Proverbs 1:2, "understanding" is "the ability to discern the difference" between spoken insights that are inconsistent with scripture and biblically consistent verbal directions that guide the parents' children into a God-focused perspective on how to live a God-honoring life, which results in the mature child becoming a person of character in a world of compromise.

57 In Proverbs, the "lazy" are described as "sluggards."

58 For example, some sluggards will excuse themselves from work by disappearing to meet "some other" need or distraction.

59 Literally, the term "parable" means: "this is that" (as in: what "this" farmer is doing in his field is an illustration of "that" heavenly truth). As a result, parables are "earthly stories that reveal heavenly truth."

60 In this age of the internet, digital opportunities, "screen" time, and social media, make a chart—on each of your children—that records each child's time invested in prayer and in studying God's Word as compared to each child's time spent/wasted on the various "screens" available to this generation of children. As a (s)parent, you may not care. As a parent, you may be "shocked" at the sparcity/sparsity of minutes invested in God as opposed to the multiplicity of hours spent/wasted on "trivial" pursuits that do not matter for eternity. In addition, what harm would it do if a parent made a weekly "work" chart for each child—with pictures next to each column describing the work the parent expects the child to perform (what a novel idea!)? On each weekly work chart, make and date a list of core tasks—such as bed-making, taking out the garbage, helping with the dishes, learning to cook, helping dad or mom with a chore, Bible devotions, prayer, picking up the room, and other age-appropriate tasks—that the child can perform or help to perform. This may help your child improve his/her work ethic, see the "growing up" years as more than a "time of privilege," and learn that life includes responsibilities.

61 One of our daughters admitted that this is what prevented her from "doing what others did" when they were teens. The prevention was the "being stronger than her strongest moment" when she was growing up by addressing every situation in her life—praising her good behavior and correcting her disobedient behavior every time possible. As a result, her parents "wore out" her desire to disobey by the time she became a teen, thus making her teen years some of the best years of her life.

62 Benjamin Spock (1903–98) was a famous secularist who rejected corporal punishment as an approved means of child discipline. He wrote such books as *The Common Sense Book of Baby and Child Care*.

63 In discipline, balance *is* needed. Society's extreme is to ignore scripture. Another extreme is the parent who inscribed the title of a hymn on the family paddle: "I Need Thee Every Hour." Refuse to "buy into" society's lie that the "time out" chair with verbal reproof is enough. Scripture approves of at least one reasonably applied method of corporal punishment: appropriately applied spanking.

64 Spoil or spank? I think of the "hesitant to spank" parent who, prior to spanking his child, said, "This hurts me more than it hurts you." The child replied, "Yes, but it hurts me in a different place." One hurt is in the heart of the parent at the disobedience of the child (as parents, we were children too—each with our own levels of disobedience/rebellion and each with our specific individual need for biblical discipline that started early and was applied often). For the child, the physical pain is a reminder that obedience to God and His authorities leads to God's best blessings. Also: when should a parent start to spank? Start young when a child responds

in obedience to spanking. When should a parent cease from spanking? When the child is old enough to be considered a young adult, which is often just after entering the teen years. In addition, with the girls—"at a certain age"—be extra careful when spanking. When applying corporal discipline, always do it in love. Always apply it appropriately—not as a beating—but as balanced/measured discipline.

65 Commonly stated: Give your child a fish and he/she will eat for a day. Teach your child to fish and he/she will eat for a lifetime. In other words, teach your child a skill—or provide a way for your child to obtain a skill—and your child should be able to feed himself/herself for a lifetime. Ignore this parental responsibility to help your child develop a skill, and your child may live to regret it. Then again, if your child refuses to "put in the effort" to learn or obtain a skill, then both the parent *and* the child may live to regret it.

66 Put another way, he/she will become a "wild child."

67 Repeated throughout this parenting manual are these words that, if implemented early and often, serve to transform insolent children into obedient offspring: "be stronger than your child's strongest moments." Biblically implemented, this "key concept" in child-raising will result in a pattern of obedience that should last beyond the parents' child-raising years.

68 In other words, as if appointed by God, become your child's disciple, for, just as discipleship is Christ's mission statement for His church (see Matthew 28:18–20), the evangelizing and discipling of your children form the mission statement of every believing parent on earth (see Ephesians 6:4 where the word *fathers* can be translated also as *parents*). As you raise your child(ren), do so in the "fear and admonition" of the Lord.

69 "Not exactly a practicing believer" and given to "idolatrous ways," Jeroboam served in Solomon's court as a highly skilled/respected construction engineer/building administrator. Although his "inheritance" did not come naturally, circumstances resulted in Jeroboam being "given" jurisdiction over the land inhabited by the ten Northern kingdoms. This was done by the population's "popular demand" (see 1 Kings 11–12).

70 In Exodus 15:25, only a tree cast into the waters could make the water sweet. It takes the "Calvary tree" of Jesus to change a child so that the mother's bitterness can become sweet. A positive "salvation relationship" with Jesus changes a child. As it does, the growth of obedience breaks out.

71 In the context of Solomon writing this passage, I wonder if Rehoboam had recently been in trouble.

72 The principles that Solomon expressed in Proverbs 19:26 still hold true today (see Ecclesiastes 1:9—"there is nothing new under the sun").

73 Applied to the local church, people in leadership must "rule their house" well (see 1 Timothy 3:5, 12). Otherwise, there is less time remaining to oversee God's congregation.

74 Anonymous.

75 Some people demand perfection. Parents need to remember that God accepts humanity. Since the cross preaches this truth, accepting humanity—with forgiveness, based on repentance—is something all of us should do.

76 The term translated *deep*, which describes the "darkness" of Proverbs 20:20 is the Hebrew word *i-son*, which describes the black center of an eyeball (the pupil), which is the part of the eye through which light comes in. If a child rejects the counsel ("light of the eye") of a parent's instruction, then that child will lack discernment, an ability to comprehend the finer nuances of life, and will walk in darkness later in life. Teach your child to listen, heed, respect, and obey the wise counsel of parents. As Jesus said, "[Since] the lamp of the body is the eye, if therefore your eye is good, your whole body will be full of light. But if your eye is bad, your whole body will be full of darkness. If therefore the light that is in you is darkness, how great *is* that darkness [indeed]" (Matthew 6:22–23). Children who do not listen to parents and "fire back" when spoken to, will, one day, submit to Jesus when "at the name of Jesus every knee should bow, of those in heaven, and of those on earth,

and of those under the earth, and *that* every tongue should confess that Jesus Christ *is* Lord, to the glory of God the Father" (Philippians 2:10–11).

77 Should a parent's will be more than a "last will and testament?" Should it be also a last will and "testimony?"

78 The Hebrew term *beten* is the term that is translated "inner depths" of his heart ("the rooms of his belly" or "the seat of a person's desires"). Interestingly, *beten* is the same term used to describe Israel's judge Ehud plunging his sword into the oversized belly (*beten*) of Moab's King Eglon, whose belly may have symbolized the gluttonous effects of Eglon living off the plunder of the people he conquered (see Judges 3:21–22). Nothing can be hidden from the "search light" of God "as even" what is hidden in a man's heart or his belly is examined and exposed by God. Since God has an "X-ray device" in heaven, we believers need to be transparent and take into the most private parts of our being only what pleases God (only what God can bless). Otherwise, the "blows" (lighter physical discipline) and "stripes" (stronger physical discipline) of corrective actions will "cleanse away" (literally: "scour" and "polish") the innermost rooms of the child's heart. As anyone who has "scoured" a kitchen sink knows, the process of cleansing is not pleasant.

79 "Your words were found, and I ate them, and Your word was to me the joy and rejoicing of my heart; for I am called by Your name, O Lord God of hosts" (Jeremiah 15:16).

80 A child can pursue "price tags" ("silver and gold") or "values" (the "favor" of God's grace). God's grace is better.

81 Since the child is "God's building," as wise master builders, what "spiritual materials" and "godly blueprint" should parents use to build on the foundation of the Lord (see 1 Corinthians 3:9–10)? Since saved children are "sanctuary saints," should parents have a say in what is allowed to enter into the "temple" which is the child's life (see 1 Corinthians 6:19–20)? If so, what does God approve concerning what enters His temple? Does He approve of the presence of unholiness, or does He approve of "what is holy" only?

82 From a sermon by Keith D. Pisani.

83 In our lifetimes, my wife and I have had hundreds of trees on our property. If all of the trees grew "straight toward the sky," every tree would have 100 percent exposure to the sun. Unfortunately, the canopy of some of the older and taller trees prevents the tops of some of the younger and shorter trees from having that direct exposure to the sun. As a result, the tops of the younger and smaller trees "bend," at an angle, away from the taller trees' canopy cover so the tops of the younger and smaller trees can have a greater exposure to the sun. It is the responsibility of believing parents to recognize that, in their child's life, there will be obstacles preventing their child from having 100 percent exposure to God's Son, Jesus. As a result, it is the parents' privilege to "bend" the child in a direction that allows that child to have a fuller exposure to God's Son. If it happens in nature with a tree and the sun, it can happen in a home with a child and "the Son," Jesus.

84 This is not an exhaustive list.

85 Everyone lives forever, in eternity. The difference in where a person lives is what that person does with Jesus. Reject Christ as Savior, and the person will spend an eternity in hell (Luke 13:3, 5). Receive Christ as Savior, and the person will spend an eternity in heaven, with Jesus (John 14:1–3, 6). Since the difference is what the child does with Jesus, encourage your child to form a salvation-relationship with Christ, at the child's earliest possible age.

86 In examining many of these Proverbs, the reader gets the impression that Solomon's "heart-pain as a parent" was self-caused due to his poor example spiritually and due to his lack of "parental investment" in the life of his son.

87 In other words, when considering involvement in societal protests or other movements, weigh the perceived advantages against the potential negative consequences—involvements and consequences that may violate God's will or scripture.

88 Although raising a child is mainly about the child, there is an aspect of child-raising that reflects back on the ability of the mom or dad to parent.

89 One of the quickest ways to lose a child's respect is to never discipline.

90 How often do these demands result in a squandering of the parents' hard-earned finances and other resources? Consider "one and done" clothing purchases, children who "do not clean their plate," or "parent-paid" college tuitions for children who refuse to "take college seriously"—wasting away education opportunities—semester by semester. Children with an "entitlement" mentality are "destroyers" (the Hebrew term *mas-hit*), which describes a self-absorbed person with an indifferent, inconsiderate, or rebellious heart who does not appreciate the value of possessions, property, anything provided, or of any other belonging—regardless of the owner or of the relationship of the provider.

91 Israel was stubborn, stuck in its ways and nonresponsive to the guidance of God (see Deuteronomy 10:16, Judges 2:19, 2 Kings 17:14, Nehemiah 9:16, Acts 7:51). For that, the nation's citizens suffered the consequences.

92 The term *delight* is the Hebrew word for "sweet delicacies, like candy" (the Hebrew term *me-ah-dah-meem*). Life will be "sweet" when a child obeys dad and mom. Also the term *soul* is a word for a person's "innermost being."

93 If Solomon did hire Agur to write Proverbs 30, then Proverbs 30:2 is significant, in the context of Solomon's perspective on his abilities to parent, when he said, "Surely I *am* more stupid than *any* man, and do not have the understanding of a man. I neither learned wisdom nor have knowledge of the Holy One" (Proverbs 30:2–3). Dare I say more about fathers who parent apart from God's guidance and help?

94 The term *filthiness* (*u-mis-so-ay-toe*) is the Hebrew term that speaks of "excrement" or "a female's uncleanness" (see Deuteronomy 23:13, Ezekiel 4:12). Dirty hearts result in dirty minds. Parents need to help their children "clean it up." Otherwise, if your children adopt the godless values of their society, God will consider their actions and attitudes as no better than the sewage and discharges rejected by all in this world—whether saved or unsaved. Yet even this "filthiness" can be washed clean by God, once the child repents (see Proverbs 30:12).

95 Since the New Testament writer mentioned "the lust of the flesh, the lust of the eyes, and the pride of life" (see 1 John 2:16), it is evident that the eye can be used for both good and evil. Post-battle, the eyes of a weakened soldier were vulnerable, as prey, to a vulture looking for a meal. However, a soldier of Christ who is spiritually "strong in the Lord" has a headpiece that preserves the eyes for future use by the Lord (see Ephesians 6:11–18). Put on the *whole* armor of God!

96 If Lemuel was Solomon, then Solomon was an adulterer; his mother, Bathsheba, was an adulteress, and his father was an adulterer. Without Christ and the indwelling Holy Spirit, how difficult would it be to overcome "that much modeled sin" in a family's history and life?

97 Unfortunately, as an adult, Rehoboam did not change. He continued along the pathway of unbelief and rebellion, losing his kingdom and his family along the way (see 2 Chronicles 10–12).

98 Even in the Creation account (in Genesis 2:4–7, 18–25), instead of creating Adam and Eve at the same time, God created Adam first and made him "wait" for the woman. Adam did "wait" to "know" Eve until they were married. Parents need to teach their sons that God's will is clear: each son must "wait" to "know" a woman until he and she are married (see 1 Thessalonians 4:3–7). Otherwise, it is immorality (the sin of fornication).

99 The greater context of Proverbs 31:1–3 is Proverbs 31:10–31 where Solomon described the perfect mother and wife: the Proverbs 31 woman who was virtuous, industrious, and pure. As everything God wanted in a woman, she was everything that Solomon was not—a role model in the home.

100 It is interesting that the Hebrew term for *excel* (the Hebrew term *a-leet*) has a connection to a "redemptive sacrifice." It is the term used of the greatest of all sacrifices that is "lifted up to the highest point on the altar"

and appreciated the most by the persons who benefited the most from the sacrifice that was made. In praising the mother (in Proverbs 31:28–29), the child is both acknowledging and appreciating the many daily and life sacrifices the mother makes so that the child can be a success. In doing so, he lifts her up to the highest place of value and honor. Praise God for godly moms!

101 Consider Solomon's unwise, self-made dilemma. Do the math: Solomon had one thousand wives and concubines. If he married his first wife at age twenty and sealed his last treaty by taking his last wife at age seventy, over that course of fifty years, Solomon would marry twenty women a year (one woman every eighteen days over a period of five decades). Did you ever wonder why Solomon described his life as being so miserable in the book of Ecclesiastes, as if his life was a "dead-end street?" If he met #222 on June 1, married her on June 8, honeymooned for a week at Aqaba on the Red Sea, carried her over his threshold on June 15 and then met wife #223 on June 16, married her on June 23, honeymooned in Lebanon (because he did Aqaba the entire previous year), returned home, and started the process again in July, it is no wonder that Solomon was miserable (too much of a good thing and too much of a bad thing result in the same conclusion: consequences)? For being the wisest man in the Old Testament, Solomon did some "really dumb" things. On occasion, so will we. One marriage—for a lifetime—is honored by God. But for Solomon, getting married was a full-time job. As a modern-day American, if Solomon got married "just to attend the receptions," some men who merely go to weddings for the meal and the cake can understand that. But, name any man—other than Solomon, a clergyman, or a justice of the peace—who would voluntarily attend twenty-plus wedding ceremonies a year. Most probably, he is the exception, not the rule. No wonder Solomon said, "Vanity of vanities … All is vanity" (Ecclesiastes 1:2).

102 As we process this wonderful passage about the Proverbs 31:10–31 "virtuous" wife/woman who applied herself "to the point of exhaustion" in her work, the reader must remember that this "multitasking" woman was more than a wife—she was the mother of multiple children. Consider her daily schedule!

103 Her beauty was not in a jar, a bottle, or in some other cosmetic container. Her beauty was in the Lord.

104 These questions are repeated in the *Parenting by the Book* small group Bible section found later in this manual on parenting.

105 Solomon began his "other" book with these words, "Vanity of vanities … all is vanity" (Ecclesiastes 1:2). That is the English translation of these Hebrew words, "*Abel of abels . . . all is abel*" (Ecclesiastes 1:2). Vanity! Emptiness! Futility! I wonder if Solomon felt better about himself when, in writing Ecclesiastes, he noticed that others in society had raised children who refused to stay off of "dead-end" streets.

106 My wife and I adopted four children. All are adults. All are living for the Lord.

107 Perhaps one of the "hidden" problems at Babel (see Genesis 11:1–9) was that, remaining in one location together, the offspring of parents were not "filling the earth." Centralized in one location were multitudes of now-grown children living at home? From a parent's point of view, although all parents love their grown children as much as they loved their children when their children were young, there is only "so much room in the basement" to house a second or third family. God wanted mankind to scatter. Instead they gathered in one place. With Genesis 2:24 in mind, other than "confusing the languages," was there more than one reason that God split the continents and scattered mankind throughout the ends of the earth (see also Genesis 10:25)? Perhaps an underlying reason for history's "first diaspora/scattering" was for mankind to obey God's first commandment to "fill/replenish" the earth through worldwide procreation.

108 One way the mother eagle upsets the nest is to place broken branches inside the nest to irritate her offspring and give them motivation to leave.

109 For a grown child to be truly independent, he/she must be autonomous and able to live apart from dad and mom. Since this principle is so important to a grown child's success, allow me to repeat this truth: true independence requires autonomy—financially, geographically, and in other ways.

110 Apart from the intervention of God's Holy Spirit to Whom all believers must yield and from Whom all believers can receive the spiritual empowerment and decision-making enablement to refuse to yield to sin, since the father's immorality ran rampant in the life of David, the "apples did not fall far from the tree." David had eight wives and many concubines (see 2 Samuel 5:13). Imagine the jealousies, lack of "true love" for David, the total dysfunction in the household, and the fractured friendships that existed among those wives and concubines. On David's deathbed, not one wife comforted him or kept him warm. Instead a local "virgin/non-wife/non-concubine"—a non-Jewish Shunammite woman named Abishag—was the woman who performed that duty (see 1 Kings 1:1–4), which begs this question: Over the years, had David's wives and concubines lost that "loving feeling" with David or had there never been "real love" in their relationships at all (were their relationships with David merely matters of convenience or had there been genuine commitment at all)? What were the names of David's sons? To whom was David married?

#1. In 1 Samuel 18:19–21, David married Saul's daughter Michal, with whom David had no biological children (did Michal have children? The writer of 2 Samuel 6:23 says no, while the same writer, in 2 Samuel 21:8 says yes! Does scripture contradict itself? No! According to 2 Samuel 21:8, Michal's children were her deceased sister Adriel's children whom Michal adopted, raised, and "brought up" as her own. Although, based on 2 Samuel 6:23, Michal had no biological children of her own, she did raise five adopted children who appropriately called her "Mom"—see 2 Samuel 21:8).

#2. According to 2 Samuel 3:2–5, during his seven-and-a-half-year reign at Hebron (the "place of fellowship"), David had Amnon, whose mother was the non-Jewish woman Ahinoam from Jezreel (it is believed that this was an arranged marriage of "political" expedience, with treaty implications).

#3. Kileab, whose mother was Abigail, who was the widow of Nabal from David's "protectorate" Carmel (2 Samuel 3:3).

#4. Absalom, whose mother was the idol-worshiper Maacah, the daughter of Talmai, who was the king of the God-denying nation of Geshur (2 Samuel 3:3).

#5. Adonijah, whose mother was Haggith, who plotted against Solomon in the context of David's death (2 Samuel 3:4).

#6. Shephatiah, of 2 Samuel 3:4, whose mother was Abital (in the original Hebrew "the daughter of the father's dew").

#7: Ithream, of 2 Samuel 3:5, whose mother was Eglah (in the Hebrew, Eglah's name means "heifer"). Although some believe that Eglah is another name for Michal, Eglah's son Ithream was never mentioned, in scripture as a blood-relative or as a direct "in-line, blood descendant" of Israel's king Saul. As a result, it makes sense that Ithream was never considered as a ranking heir to David's throne.

Then, #8: in 2 Samuel 12:24, David married Uriah's wife, Bathsheba, with whom David had a son, Solomon, and three other sons (Shimea, Shobab, and Nathan). In total, David had six sons in Hebron, four sons by Bathsheba, one daughter (Tamar), and at least ten other sons by various other women (see 1 Chronicles 3:4–7). Imagine the sibling rivalries that flared up in that home—especially when it is evident that father/parent David was absent "emotionally" for most of the time as he cared for his kingdom at the expense of his home.

111 As parents, make sure your children know: family counts! "Family first!" Family is important!

112 Here is a sensitive subject that raises emotions in most parents, regardless of their view(s). The endnoted statement from Jonah 4:11 may beg the question: Is there an age of accountability before which a child is considered "under the blood" and does not yet "need" to receive Christ as Savior? On the existence of an age of accountability, there are at least two views: View #1): There is no age of accountability and every person, regardless of age, must "repent of their sins" and "receive Jesus Christ as Savior" in order to go to heaven (see Romans 3:10, 23; 5:6–8; 6:23; 10:9-10; John 1:12; Titus 3:5–6; 1 John 5:11–13). This view is based, in part, on passages such as John 3:3, 7 where Christ said, "Ye must be born again (born from above; born from heaven) and Romans 10:9–10 where a person, to be saved, must "confess with his mouth that Jesus Christ is Lord and believe in his heart that God has raised Him from the dead." Those who do not believe in an age of accountability would say that babies are not saved because babies cannot meet the "response" requirements of the aforementioned passages. View #2): There is an age of accountability before which a child can go to heaven prior to receiving Christ as Savior (including unborn babies who were miscarried or aborted) but, when that child reaches his/her age of accountability, that child must repent of his/her sins and receive Christ as Savior in order to go to heaven. What scripture passages are used to defend the existence of an age of accountability? A): Matthew 19:14. "But Jesus said, Suffer [the] little children, and forbid them not, to come unto me: for of such is the kingdom of heaven." Since pre-adults in Christ's day were, "[as such, [of] the kingdom of heaven," then are modern-day pre-adults—prior to reaching an age of accountability—[of] the kingdom of heaven, as well? B): 2 Samuel 12:23. When David's offspring from Bathsheba died (at eight days old or younger), David said, "I shall go to him, but he will not return to me" (2 Samuel 12:23). When he died, where did David go? He went to the "House of the Lord" (see Psalm 23:6) which, in the Old Testament was Paradise/Upper Sheol and in the church age, it is heaven (see Ephesians 4:4–8, where Christ carried captivity captive, and Revelation 21, 22, which describes the new heaven). Is it possible that David knew that he would see his baby, in eternity, in the House of the Lord (heaven)? C): In contrast, in 2 Samuel 18:33, when David's full-grown (adult) son Absalom died, David lamented, wept, and said, "O my son, Absalom! Absalom! My son, Absalom! If only I had died, instead of you! O Absalom. My son! My son!" (2 Samuel 18:33). Why was David less upset at losing his baby than he was at losing his full-grown son, Absalom? Is it possible that David's infant son was under his age of accountability while David's full-grown son—who had rejected a relationship with God—had reached his age of accountability and was "held eternally accountable" for his sins. Is it safe to assume that, in eternity, David would see one son but not the other? C: Jonah 4:11, Isaiah 7:16. If there is an age of accountability, at what age does a child reach it? In Jonah 4:11, when Nineveh repented and was saved, in that city alone, there were 120,000 children who could not "discern between their right hand and their left hand." In addition, in the context of Isaiah's prophesy concerning a baby born of a virgin (see Isaiah 7:14, 16), a child named Maher-shalal-hash-baz was born who had not yet reached the age where he could "know to refuse the evil, and choose the good," which is modern society's definition of the age of accountability (the age at which a child can discern between what is good and what is evil). By connecting Isaiah 7:16 with Jonah 4:11, is the age of accountability "at or around" the age when a child can distinguish between his/her right hand and his/her left hand? If it is, then parents need to give a clear presentation of the gospel to each child "at or around" the age when each can child can discern between hands. This begs several other questions: Prior to the age when a child can discern this, can a child be saved by receiving Jesus Christ as Savior? Absolutely, yes! From personal experience, my wife and several of our children were saved prior to the age when they could discern their right hand from their left hand (my wife was saved at the age of four and my children were saved "at or around" that age. Each, as an adult, bases their salvation on their "salvation decision" at those young ages). Also, having overseen children as a head of school(s), having taught children as a physical education teacher, having been a pastor of

churches with young children in attendance, and having had four children of our own, I've found it interesting that children not only "receive Christ as Savior/come to Christ" at different ages but children also discern the difference between their hands at different ages, depending on the child. Some children at age four (K4, K5) know the difference between their right hand and left hand. In contrast, some children in second grade (at age seven) do not know the difference. As a result, is it possible that, when a child discerns the difference between his/her hands that this is "his/her age" when the parent or other believer should "make sure" that this child is given a clear gospel presentation and a specific opportunity to receive Jesus Christ as Savior? In conclusion, is there or is there not an age of accountability before which a child does/does not need to "repent" of his/her sins and "receive" Jesus Christ as Savior? Also, for those who believe in eternal security, if a child must receive Christ as Savior when arriving at the age of accountability, did that same child "lose" his/her salvation at the moment/day that child arrived at his/her age of accountability? There are some truths that only God knows. When we, as believers, get to heaven we will have the privilege of "looking around" heaven. If miscarried and aborted babies are there, and if offspring are there who died when they were younger children, we will know that there was an age of accountability. If not, it is a great idea to share Christ with your children at the earliest possible age so each might be sure of their salvation-relationship with Jesus.

113 The author, Keith D. Pisani, has a published follow-up book for children entitled *Jesus Loves Me: A Follow-Up Guide for Children*. It is available through Westbow Press, online, or through the author's ministry website: www.keithpisaniministries.com.

114 In addition, Titus 2:3–5 describes the responsibility of the older women to teach the younger women and girls about spiritual disciplines and godly values. Titus 2:6–8 describes the responsibility of the older men to teach the younger men and boys about spiritual disciplines and godly values. These teachings are included in Paul's admonition to the island of Crete's "Teaching Pastor" (Titus), in Titus 2:1, who was told to speak the things that become "sound doctrine," which, in the language in which the New Testament was written, is the translation of two Greek words: (1) the term *ugiainouse*, which is the root for the English word *hygiene*, and (2) the term *didaskalia*, which is the Greek word most often translated as "teaching(s)." Used together, the terms describe teachings that "lack sickness-causing germs" and are "wholesome" and "healthy" for those who receive those teachings. Hand-me-down clothes may be despised by some, but healthy and biblically consistent "hand-me-down" instructions concerning life and values are honored by the Lord. Included in these "hand-me-down" values are Spirit control (Titus 2:4), loving relationships (Titus 2:4), right responses (Titus 2:5), biblical morality (Titus 2:5), kindness (Titus 2:5), a high regard for leadership in the home (Titus 2:5), respect for God's Word (Titus 2:5), self-control (Titus 2:6), and how to have a godly testimony as a biblical example to others both inside and outside the home (Titus 2:7–8). When they come of age as adults, children who learn these lessons will do more than respect God and His Word. When older, they will enjoy a relationship of mutual love, mutual respect, and mutual friendship for as long as each will live.

115 These questions are repeated in the "Parenting by the Book" Small Group Bible Section found later in this manual on parenting.

116 Were Cain and Abel twins, or was Abel born after Cain was weaned?

117 While acknowledging God's commandment to "be fruitful and multiply," this question is in light of Eve's potential frustration with her first son, Cain, which may have resulted in the conception and birth of Eve's second son, Abel.

Printed in the United States
By Bookmasters